AJILYA DUROJI

If You Can Go, Then Go

A Black Woman's Guide to Moving Abroad for Safety, Peace, and a Softer Life

DUROJI
PUBLISHING

For every Black woman who ever felt unsafe in her own neighborhood.
For every brother who's been told to shrink himself just to survive.
For every sister who dared to dream of peace, even when the world told her it was too much.
For the aunties, the cousins, the elders, and the babies who deserve more than struggle.
This book is for you.
May it remind you that your safety, your joy, and your freedom are not luxuries. They are your birthright.

"Staying where you're disrespected is not loyalty, it's self-abandonment. Go where your life is valued and your peace is protected."

Ajilya Duroji

Contents

Foreword   iii

Preface   iv

Acknowledgments   vi

Prologue   1

Introduction   3

Chapter 1: Why Leave? Why Now?   8

Chapter 2: Funding Your Freedom (Even If You're Not Rich)   17

Chapter 3: Visas, Paperwork & the FinePrint   32

Chapter 4: Top Countries to Consider (And Why)   51

Chapter 5: Creating a Soft Life Abroad (Without Apology)   114

Chapter 6: Navigating Culture Shock & Settling In   120

Chapter 7: Raising Children Abroad (Family Freedom)   132

Chapter 8: Retiring Abroad (Freedom Isn't Just for the...   142

Chapter 9: Love, Dating & Relationships Abroad   151

Chapter 10: Safety, Boundaries & Thriving on Your Own Terms   160

Chapter 11: Move Abroad and Enjoy the Good Life   167

Chapter 12: Your First 90 Days Abroad   181

Chapter 13: Mistakes That Cost You — and How to Avoid Them   186

Chapter 14: Building a Location-Independent Life Long- Term   193

Chapter 15: Before You Go — Smart Tips & Tidbits   199

Chapter 16: Being Black Abroad — Culture, Colorism & Feeling...   204

Appendix: Resource List   212

Final Word   219

Conclusion   221

Epilogue   223

Afterword   224

Foreword

This book isn't theory. It's not a fairy tale about "living abroad." It's real talk for Black women and men tired of being told to settle for less. We know what it feels like to constantly fight to be respected, to stay alert in spaces where your safety, dignity, and peace are not guaranteed. If you picked up this book, chances are you're already thinking about leaving that behind.

I wrote this book because I got tired of watching people I love pour all their energy into surviving systems designed to break them. I also got tired of the Instagram version of moving abroad-perfect beaches, cocktails, and #expatlife with no mention of visas, paperwork, culture shock, or the racism that sometimes follows us across borders. That's not the whole story; you deserve the truth before making life-changing decisions.

This book is your starting point. It gives you the tools, the warnings, and the step-by-step guidance to move smart, not desperate. I'm not here to convince anyone to leave. Stay if you're safe, respected, and at peace where you are. But if you've been feeling the pull to go and know your soul is screaming for more, this book will help you prepare with both eyes open.

I'm speaking directly to you as a sister, someone who's lived it, and someone who believes your life is worth more than survival mode. Take what serves you, apply it to your situation, and start building a life where your freedom, joy, and safety are non-negotiable.

Let's get into it.

Preface

When I first started planning to leave the United States, I didn't have a road map. I had Google, a few random Facebook groups, and a lot of mixed messages. Some people swore moving abroad would fix everything. Others told me I was crazy even to try. What I didn't find was a resource written for people like me, Black, tired of survival mode, and ready to create a softer, safer life.

This book grew out of my own journey. Every page comes from lived experience, hard lessons, and the things I wish someone had told me before I booked a flight. I've been through culture shock, gatekeeping, scams, loneliness, and the joy of finding real community. I've seen what happens when you move unprepared and the freedom that comes when you do it right.

This is not a fantasy book. I'm not here to sell you palm trees and pina coladas. I'm here to give you the truth: the paperwork, the money, the safety concerns, the culture shifts, and the reality of being Black abroad. Some of it will be uncomfortable, but all of it is necessary.

You'll find step-by-step guides, personal stories, and checklists that make the process less overwhelming. You'll also see the bigger picture, why so many of us are leaving right now, and how living abroad can be about more than escape. It can be about choosing peace, dignity, and possibility.

I didn't write this to convince anyone. If you're good where you are, stay. But if you've been feeling that pull and asking yourself, "What if?" this book is for you. It's the resource I wish I had, and I hope it helps you move with clarity, confidence, and courage.

Acknowledgments

This book didn't happen in a vacuum. It came together because of the people who showed up, supported me, and reminded me that telling the truth matters.

To the Black women and men who shared their stories of moving abroad, you gave me perspective, courage, and the receipts that this life is possible. Thank you for being open, honest, and unfiltered.

To my family and friends who listened to me repeatedly talk about visas, flights, and starting over, you kept me grounded when I wanted to give up.

To the expat communities that welcomed me instead of shutting me out, thank you for proving that true community is possible across borders.

Thank you, too, to those who tried to gate-keep or block the way. You pushed me to carve out my lane and create resources that don't exclude people like me.

Most importantly, to our ancestors, the ones who were chained, displaced, and denied freedom of movement, the ones who couldn't choose where to live, how to love, or how to dream. I carry you with me on every page of this book. This work is for you and because of you.

And to every reader holding this book: thank you. You are why I wrote this. Whether you're still dreaming, planning, or living abroad, your presence here means you're serious about your future. I don't take that lightly.

This book is my offering to you. May your passport always open doors, not close them.

Ajilya

Prologue

Too many of us live in a nightmare and pretend it's normal.

Every time I turned on the news, scrolled through social media, or listened to stories from friends, I saw the same pattern: Black women and men being harassed, disrespected, and pushed to the edge in places we're supposed to call home. From hospitals mistreating Black mothers, to police terrorizing our neighborhoods, to random strangers bold enough to spit hate in our faces, this is the reality we're living in.

At some point, I had to ask myself the tricky question: *Do I want to survive here, or do I want to live somewhere else where survival isn't the whole story?*

That's what this book is about. It's not a fantasy guide to sipping cocktails on a beach. It's about the real, practical, messy, and life-changing process of moving abroad for safety, peace, and a softer life.

I've experienced the confusion, culture shock, gatekeeping, and loneliness. I've also experienced the joy of finding community, the relief of walking streets without fear, and the calm of living in a place where my life feels like mine again.

This book is for the ones who are ready. I'm not here to convince you to go. I'm here to give you the tools, the stories, and the reality checks so you can make the move if that's what your spirit is calling for. If you feel safe, respected, and free where you are, stay. But if you're tired of settling for crumbs, know there's a bigger table waiting for you somewhere else.

This is not about escape. It's about choice. And for the first time in generations, we have it.

If you can go, then go.

Introduction

Let me get this out of the way up front: This book does not beg you to leave the United States, the U.K., or anywhere else. It was written for people who are already thinking about it, already tired, already planning, and already searching for what's next.

If you feel safe where you are, if you're respected where you live, if your life feels steady and full, then this book isn't for you. Stay where your soul feels good. No one should have to convince you to save your own ass, and I'm not about to try.

But if you're reading this because you feel stuck, unsafe, under constant stress, or worn down by systems that don't value your life, then you're in the right place. You already know why you're here. You need tools, clarity, and someone to tell you the truth about what moving abroad is like. That's what I'm giving you.

Here's what this book will do:

- Break down the "why" behind leaving, including the social and political realities pushing many of us to go.
- Show you how to prepare financially, emotionally, and practically.
- Walk you through visas, paperwork, and the fine print that trips people up.
- Give you an honest look at top countries and cities to consider, including how safe, welcoming, and affordable they are for Black folks and LGBTQ expats.

- Share my personal experiences with culture shock, community, and building a new life abroad.
- Provide tools, checklists, and stories to help you avoid the expensive mistakes people make when they don't plan right.

This isn't a fantasy. Moving abroad won't fix everything, and it won't always be easy. But it can give you options that many of our ancestors never had. That's why I wrote this: so you don't waste time, money, or energy figuring things out the hard way.

Think of this book as your guide and your permission slip. If your gut has been whispering or screaming that it's time to go, I'm here to say you're not crazy. You're not wrong. You don't have to settle for less than safety, peace, and a softer life.

So let's get into it.

Let me get this out of the way up front: I didn't write this book to beg you to leave the United States, the U.K., or anywhere else. I wrote it for the people who are already thinking about it, already tired, already planning, and already searching for what's next.

If you feel safe where you are, if you're respected where you live, if your life feels steady and full, then this book isn't for you. Stay where your soul feels good. No one should have to convince you to save your own ass, and I'm not about to try.

But if you're reading this because you feel stuck, unsafe, under constant stress, or worn down by systems that don't value your life, then you're in the right place. You already know why you're here. You need tools, clarity, and someone to tell you the truth about what moving abroad is like. That's what I'm giving you.

Here's what this book will do:

- Break down the "why" behind leaving, including the social and political realities pushing many of us to go.
- Show you how to prepare financially, emotionally, and practically.
- Walk you through visas, paperwork, and the fine print that trips people up.
- Give you an honest look at top countries and cities to consider, including how safe, welcoming, and affordable they are for Black folks and LGBTQ expats.
- Share my personal experiences with culture shock, community, and building a new life abroad.
- Provide tools, checklists, and stories to help you avoid the expensive mistakes people make when they don't plan right.

This isn't a fantasy. Moving abroad won't fix everything, and it won't always be easy. But it can give you options that many of our ancestors never had. That's why I wrote this: so you don't waste time, money, or energy figuring things out the hard way.

Think of this book as your guide and your permission slip. If your gut has been whispering or screaming that it's time to go, I'm here to say you're not crazy. You're not wrong. You don't have to settle for less than safety, peace, and a softer life.

So let's get into it.

* * *

The Moment Everything Changed: My Personal Reason for Moving Abroad

In 2021, something in me shifted.

On paper, I had it all—a six-figure remote job. Grown kids thriving. No debt. No food insecurity. I could buy what I wanted, travel when I felt like it, and check off all the boxes of "success." But my gut kept saying: it's time for you to leave.

It made no sense. I had cake-walked through COVID, stacking money from the comfort of my home. I wasn't running from a crisis. I wasn't forced out. Still, the feeling wouldn't let me go. By November of that year, I gave in.

For those who believe in spiritual awakenings, I lived one. I started seeing things differently. My intuition went into overdrive. I'd wake up at 1:11, then 3:33, then 4:44. I thought I was losing my damn mind. But deep down, I knew something bigger than me was calling. So I listened. I packed up, put my life in storage, and left the country. There was no master plan. There was no research. It was just me, my gut, and a one-way ticket.

It sounds wild, I know. But I wasn't the only one. I've met others with stories just like mine, people who felt grabbed by the gut and guided abroad for reasons they couldn't explain at the time.

Moving abroad became the most transformative decision of my life. And let me keep it real: It wasn't easy. I learned the hard way what happens after the beach photos fade. I had to figure out how to make money without leaning on a U.S. job. I had to learn what it means to start fresh in a place where nothing was familiar.

But here's the truth:
The freedom came with struggle.

6

The beauty came with breakdowns.
The peace came with paperwork.

And it was all worth it.

How to Use This Book

This guide is here to meet you exactly where you are, whether you're just beginning to daydream about moving abroad, knee-deep in visa research, or quietly stacking your savings for an exit plan you haven't told anyone about yet.

Each chapter blends the practical with the personal. You'll find clear steps, tools, country insights, journal prompts, affirmations, and questions meant to stir your spirit. Because leaving the country is more than a checklist, it's a healing process. A shedding. A shift

There's no right way to use this book. Read it front to back, or jump to the chapters that speak directly to your current season.

But as you turn these pages, I hope you remember this:

You are not just moving. You are reclaiming your peace. You are choosing your joy.

You are rewriting your life.

And you don't have to do it alone.

Chapter 1: Why Leave? Why Now?

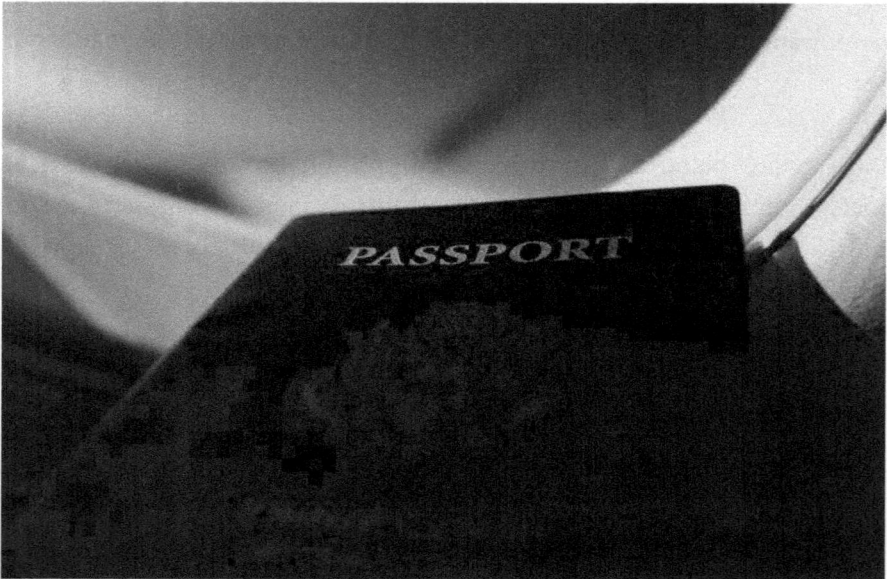

For many of us, the decision to leave is not just about burnout but survival. When you're raising Black children in a system that doesn't see their full humanity, when you're navigating hospitals that ignore your pain, when your very existence is met with suspicion, the idea of peace becomes more than a dream. It becomes a need.

There comes a moment when "making it work" just doesn't work anymore.

Maybe it's the job that leaves you drained. Perhaps it's the news cycles full of Black death and no justice. Maybe it's watching your child having to endure mass shooting drills, or shrinking themselves in school to stay safe. Perhaps it's the quiet terror that one mistake could become a hashtag.

You may have done everything "right"—climbed the ladder, kept the peace, raised the kids, paid the bills—and still wonder: Is this all there is?

Sometimes, freedom doesn't look like a protest or a plot twist. It seems like finally listening to your body when it whispers, "Rest."

Sometimes it's the moment you stop settling for "fine."

Moving abroad isn't just about chasing adventure. For many of us, it's about survival, peace of mind, and dignity. Black women and men are weighing the risks of staying versus the possibilities of leaving because the threats at home are no longer hypothetical. They are real, present, and growing.

Signs It May Be Time to Leave

Here are a few soul-honest indicators that it might be time for a radical shift:

- You no longer feel safe walking, driving, or in public spaces.
- Your children are facing racism in schools that is ignored or excused. You've experienced medical neglect or bias during critical moments, like childbirth.
- New policies or quiet discrimination threaten your job or housing security.
- You notice your mental health suffering under constant stress and vigilance.
- You're constantly exhausted, and Rest never seems to refill you. You're numbing out more than you're tuning in.

- You've outgrown your environment, and your world has shrunk.
- You've been called "too sensitive," "too much," or "ungrateful" for desiring peace and purpose.
- You no longer recognize the person in the mirror.

For some, the question is no longer "Should I go?" but "How much longer can I endure this?"

If any of these resonate, take a breath. You're not broken. You're awakening.

Firsthand perspective

Latoya, 42, Teacher "I wasn't running from something as much as I was running toward myself. I had a good job in Atlanta, but came home feeling invisible daily. I visited Mérida, Mexico, for a friend's wedding and couldn't believe the difference; neighbors greeted me, strangers offered help, and I wasn't followed around in stores. Within six months, I moved. My anxiety dropped, my health improved, and for the first time in years, I could breathe."

Monique, 35, IT Consultant, "My trigger was safety. After a break-in at my apartment, the police response made it clear I wasn't a priority. I researched countries with lower violent crime rates and strong Black expat networks. Portugal kept coming up. I visited Lisbon, joined a Facebook expat group, and realized I could keep my U.S. job while living there. A year later, I'm paying half my old rent, walking home at night without fear, and building friendships I never thought I'd find."

Current Threats and Social Drivers

Since late 2024, events in both the U.S. and the U.K. have intensified the urgency of leaving. These aren't abstract theories. They're happening in real time, and they're happening to us.

Racial Violence and Lynching-Style Deaths

- In Mississippi, 21-year-old Demartravion "Trey" Reed was found hanging from a tree on his college campus in September 2025. Police claimed no foul play, but his family and civil rights advocates are demanding answers, given the state's history of lynching.
- In Alabama, Dennoriss Richardson, who had accused police of brutality, was found hanging in late 2024. Officials called it suicide, but the staging and the history of racial terror in the region sparked public outcry.

These cases echo America's darkest history and remind Black families that we are still not safe from racial violence dressed up as coincidence.

Case Study: Community in Fear

When Trey Reed was found, his classmates described living in constant fear. Some stopped walking alone at night. Others began planning transfers to schools in different states. His case reminded young Black students that racial terror is not history, it's present.

Reflection: If seeing us hanging from trees in 2025 doesn't shake you, nothing will. This is why some of us refuse to wait around.

White Supremacy and Hate Campaigns

In the U.S., men tied to neo-Nazi groups have been arrested for threatening to kill Black and Jewish communities. In the U.K., over 110,000 people joined a far-right rally in London in September 2025, where racist and anti-immigrant rhetoric was shouted from the stage.

Online platforms still host extremist calls for violence against minorities, spreading fear faster than authorities can respond.

This isn't Satire anymore. White supremacist threats are loud, public, and emboldened.

Reflection: When people are bold enough to plot our harm out loud, the warning is clear. You either take it seriously or gamble with your life.

Everyday Harassment in Public

It's not only the high-profile cases that remind us we're at risk. Every day, harassment of Black and Brown men, women, and children in public has escalated. Families report being followed in stores, stopped without cause, and targeted with slurs on public transit. Videos flood social media of kids being bullied at school, mothers being harassed in parks, and men being threatened for simply existing in the "wrong" neighborhood.

Case Study: A Child on the Bus

In March 2025, a video went viral from Georgia showing a Black middle schooler being taunted with racial slurs on the school bus. Other kids laughed while the driver ignored it. The child's mother said her son came home shaking, asking why no one stood up for him. That moment was a turning point for her; she began looking into relocation abroad, saying, "If my child can't ride a bus in peace, I need to find somewhere he can."

Case Study: Harassed on the Train

In July 2025, a Black woman commuting on a London train recorded a group of men shouting racist slurs at her while others looked away. She reported that no one intervened when she asked for help from staff. Later, she said, "The silence hurt more than the insults. It told me I was on my own." That experience pushed her to start exploring a move to Ghana, where she had family roots and felt her dignity might be safer

Reflection: If this feels familiar, you don't need convincing; you already know the time.

Mistreatment in Healthcare

Black mothers continue to face what researchers call "obstetric racism." Hospitals have ignored cries for help during childbirth, with some cases ending in preventable deaths. In Virginia, a neonatal nurse was arrested after multiple premature infants were found with unexplained injuries. Among the affected were Black babies. Families also report being dismissed, mocked, or even taunted by nurses when requesting dignity and safety for themselves and their newborns.

Case Study: A Mother's Story

In 2025, a Black mother in California reported that nurses ignored her repeated calls for help during labor. Her pain was dismissed as "exaggeration," and by the time staff intervened, her child was in distress. She survived, but the trauma of being unheard has stayed with her.

Reflection: If we can't even give birth without fearing for our lives or our babies, then the system is broken. Please don't wait for it to fix itself.

Policy RollBacks and Legal Threats

In the U.S., the incoming administration has aligned with "Project 2025," a far-right plan to dismantle civil rights protections, diversity programs, and agencies that enforce anti-discrimination laws. States continue to pass laws targeting education, voting rights, and diversity efforts, policies that disproportionately strip protections from Black communities. In the U.K., hate incidents and racist attacks have surged, while far-right groups push to tighten immigration and limit multicultural expression.

Case Study: A Professional's Choice

A mid-level manager in Georgia decided to leave the U.S. after her company's diversity program was shut down under new state restrictions. "It was like they were telling us, 'We don't want you here, not even in the workplace,'" she said. She moved to Portugal in 2025, continuing her career remotely and reporting feeling more valued and safe.

Reflection: When laws start peeling away your rights individually, you don't argue about "maybe." You decide how much you're willing to risk by staying.

Why Now Matters

You might feel torn between staying and fighting or leaving and building anew. Both are valid choices, but timing matters. Waiting until laws are fully rolled back, violence escalates further, or medical neglect becomes a crisis could cost lives, money, and peace of mind. Leaving now doesn't mean giving up. It means choosing safety, health, and a softer life before circumstances force you into survival mode.

My Takeaway Regarding Current Threats and Social Drivers

When I say "Why leave? Why now?" this is what I mean: we are living in a moment where hate has resurged, policies are regressing, and the dignity of Black women and men is under daily threat. Staying is not neutral. It comes with costs to your body, mind, and spirit. The decision to go abroad is no longer just a dream. For many, it's becoming the most practical response to the rising dangers we face.

Radical Relocation as a Healing Tool

Leaving isn't always an escape. Sometimes, it's an arrival at your true self.

Radical relocation isn't about fantasy. It's about re-centering your joy and safety. A new country won't magically fix everything, but it can offer:

- A lower cost of living reduces your financial stress.
- More time and space to explore your creativity, Rest, and desires
- A slower pace of life that honors your nervous system
- Cultural values that affirm family, beauty, community, or spiritual growth
- A chance to step outside the systems that have been slowly eroding your spirit

For many women, moving abroad becomes the first time they feel safe enough to exhale.

The Myth of "Giving Up"

Choosing yourself is not quitting. It's not failure. It's not selfish. It's sacred.

We live in a world that glorifies grit but often punishes softness. Choosing ease can feel radical, even rebellious if you've been taught that your worth is tied to struggle.

But hear this:

You are not giving up. You are breaking free.

This book is about helping you recognize your power to choose differently. Choose a life that doesn't require you to shrink, harden, or hustle every hour of the day.

Because you were made for more than survival, you were made for liberation.

Emotional Exit vs. Strategic Exit

Leaving because you're fed up is different from going with a plan. An emotional exit looks like quitting your job, packing a suitcase, and hoping it works out. A strategic exit means preparing your finances, paperwork, and support system before you leave. Both may get you on a plane, but only one keeps you abroad without burning out.

Reflection Prompt:

- What part of my life feels the most unsustainable right now?
- What's missing from my current reality when I picture my ideal day?
- Who told me I had to stay, and do I still believe them?
- What would choosing myself look like today?

Your answers don't need to be perfect. They need to be honest. And from that honesty, a new life can begin.

Affirmation:

"I am not imagining this pressure — I am awakening to truth."

Chapter 2: Funding Your Freedom (Even If You're Not Rich)

Let's break a myth: You do not need a trust fund, a sugar daddy, or a viral startup to leave the country and create a life you love.

You need clarity, creativity, and a willingness to see beyond the traditional 9-to-5 income model.

Money doesn't have to be a wall. It can be a bridge.

This chapter is your financial flashlight, shining light on what's possible, even if you don't have enough.

Step 1: Build Your Freedom Fund (Emergency Savings + Transition Budget)

Your Freedom Fund is not just savings, it's sacred preparation. It's your proof to yourself that you're serious. It's your safety net and your soft landing.

What to include in your transition budget:

- Flight(s)
- Visa application fees
- First month's rent + deposit
- Shipping/storage of your belongings (if applicable)
- Short-term stay (Airbnb/hotel) for the arrival period
- Language learning apps or tutors
- Legal and document prep (apostilles, notarizations, etc.)
- Portable tech (laptop, chargers, power adapters)
- Health insurance for expats (initial coverage)
- Emergency fund: at least 3–6 months of living expenses in your destination country

Pro Tip: Open a separate high-yield savings account and automate transfers each payday, even if it's just $25. Watch your escape route grow.

Step 2: Rethink How You Make Money (Remote Work, Freelancing, and Passive Income)

A job doesn't have to be local to pay the bills. In fact, many people fund their international life by working online while living in low-cost countries.

Remote Work Ideas:

- Virtual Assistant
- Project Management
- Customer Service Rep
- Tech Support
- Online Teaching (ESL, tutoring, test prep)
- Remote HR/Admin roles

Freelance/Contract Work:

- Writing / Editing Graphic Design
- Social Media Management Web Development
- Digital Marketing
- Translation Services

Passive or Location-Independent Income Streams:

- Digital Products (eBooks, courses, templates)
- Print-on-Demand merchandise
- YouTube or Podcast monetization
- Affiliate Marketing
- Rental Income (Airbnb your U.S. property)
- Dividend-paying investments

Websites to Start Exploring:

- Upwork.com Fiverr.com
- Remote.co
- WeWorkRemotely.com
- FlexJobs.com
- Teachable, Gumroad (for creating/selling digital products)

Pro Tip: You don't need to be an "expert." You need to solve a problem. Start with what you already know how to do.

Protecting Your Remote Work & Online Access Abroad

What is a VPN service?

- A VPN (Virtual Private Network) creates a secure, encrypted connection between your device and the internet.
- It hides your real IP address and location.
- It protects your data from hackers and surveillance.
- It helps you access geo-blocked websites or services (like streaming or banking apps restricted to your home country).

Top VPN services for expats:

- ExpressVPN: Fast, reliable, easy to use. Works well with streaming and secure browsing.
- NordVPN: Strong security features, many servers worldwide, good for
- Privacy.
- Surfshark: Affordable, unlimited device connections, strong privacy tools.
- CyberGhost: User-friendly, suitable for streaming and privacy.
- Private Internet Access (PIA): Strong security, many servers, and customization.

What is a VPN router?

- A VPN router has VPN software built in or configured to connect all devices on your home network through a VPN.
- This means every device connected to the router uses the VPN automatically.
- It protects devices that don't support VPN apps directly, like smart TVs or game consoles.
- It helps avoid setting up a VPN individually on every device.

Top VPN routers or router-compatible VPNs:

- Asus routers (models like RT-AC86U, RT-AX88U) support VPN installation.
- Netgear Nighthawk series can be configured for VPN.
- Linksys routers often support VPN setups.
- Many VPN services offer guides on configuring their VPN on these routers.

How to use a VPN service while living abroad:

1. Choose a trusted VPN provider and subscribe.
2. Download and install the VPN app on your devices (phone, laptop, tablet).
3. Open the app, log in, and connect to a server in your home country or desired location.
4. Use the internet as usual, with your data encrypted and your location masked.
5. Disconnect when you no longer need the VPN.

How to use a VPN router:

1. Buy a router that supports VPN or flash compatible firmware (like DD-WRT or Tomato).

2. Subscribe to a VPN service that supports router configuration.
3. Follow the VPN provider's step-by-step guide to set up the VPN on your router.
4. Connect your devices to this VPN router's Wi-Fi or Ethernet.
5. All traffic from connected devices will route through the VPN automatically.

* * *

Lesson Learned the Hard Way

Let me keep it all the way honest with you.

When I first left the U.S., I had a six-figure job—the legal way. My employer gave me the green light to work abroad remotely, and I thought I had it made. I was grateful. I thought, if I keep killing it, go above and beyond, and be a loyal team player, they'll have my back, too.

Wrong.

Two years later, two weeks before Christmas, they ended my contract. No warning. No cushion.

Just done.

Because I hadn't planned for this type of hit, my whole life abroad became shaky fast.

And here's the truth nobody wants to say: long gone are the days when hard work and dedication earned you employer loyalty. These companies don't give two shits about you, your family, your kids, or your well-being. You are a line item on a spreadsheet; the only thing that matters to them is the bottom line. Your hard work feeds their profits; anything beyond that is not their problem. All those years of fucking code-switching, making yourself smaller, keeping it "professional"?

A damn sham.

Whether you stay in the States or pack your bags and bounce, you're going to have to figure out how to save your own ass. My biggest mistake was betting my freedom abroad on a U.S. paycheck without a backup plan. I should have had a side hustle, emergency savings, and something that was mine, not tied to a boss or a budget line.

The lesson? Don't wait for a layoff, a contract cut, or a "company restructuring" email to figure out how you'll eat next month. The day you decide to move abroad, you should start building multiple income streams. Your peace abroad should never rest in the hands of one paycheck.

* * *

Plan B Income Checklist

Because loyalty doesn't pay the bills if the job disappears.

1. Build at Least One Independent Income Stream

- Freelance skills (writing, design, consulting, teaching online)
- List item #2Digital products (eBooks, courses, templates)
- Affiliate marketing or brand partnerships
- Remote contract work not tied to one client.

2. Create a 3–6 Month Emergency Fund

- Cover rent, food, insurance, and visa renewal costs
- Keep it in an accessible international account, not just a U.S. bank.
-

3. Diversify Where Your Money Comes From?

- Aim for at least two different clients or income channels.
- Mix short-term and long-term contracts for stability

4. Protect Yourself Legally & Financially

- Check your visa type. Does it allow other work?
- Keep a local bank account and an online banking option (Wise, Revolut)

5. Build Skills That Travel With You

- Choose work you can do from anywhere (and for anyone)
- Keep upgrading your skill set so you can pivot fast if needed

6. Have a 'Quick Cash' Plan

- List 3–5 things you can start doing within 2 weeks to earn money
- Examples: tutoring English, social media management, selling a service

Reminder: Don't get comfortable with just one source of income, especially if it's a U.S.-based job. Your freedom abroad deserves a safety net.

Step 3: Make Your Money Stretch in Low-Cost Countries

The same $2,000 that barely covers rent in a U.S. city can fund a whole, abundant life abroad.

Budget breakdown in a low-cost country (e.g., Mexico, Thailand, Ecuador):

Country	Rent (1BR)	Utilities + Internet	Groceries	Transportation	Health Insurance	Fun/Misc	Total Monthly
Mexico (Mérida)	$500	$80	$200	$40	$60	$200	$1,080
Portugal (Porto)	$750	$120	$250	$60	$80	$250	$1,510
Thailand (Chiang Mai)	$400	$50	$150	$30	$50	$150	$830
Ghana (Accra)	$700	$100	$300	$60	$100	$200	$1,460

Tip: The amount is subject to change. Remember to factor in flights home, currency exchange rates, and inflation.

Top Low-Cost Countries to Explore:

- Mexico
- Thailand
- Portugal
- Ecuador
- Colombia
- Vietnam

- Georgia (the country)
- Albania

Each offers residency pathways, affordable healthcare, and vibrant expat communities.

Banking Abroad Made Easy

Fam, I learned quickly that you can have all the tax breaks in the world, but you're in trouble if you can't access your money. Choosing the right bank and credit cards before you leave can save you hundreds (or thousands) every year.

Why Charles Schwab is the Immigrant Expat's BFF

- No foreign ATM fees. They refund all those sneaky charges other banks hit you with when you withdraw cash abroad.
- Global acceptance. Your Schwab debit card works almost anywhere Visa is accepted.
- Great exchange rates. No 3% "foreign transaction" nonsense.
- Easy online management. No "come into the branch" foolishness when on another continent.

How to use it:

1. Open a Schwab High Yield Investor Checking account before you leave the U.S. (must be linked to a Schwab brokerage account, which is free)
2. Keep a small balance in checking, and transfer only what you need weekly; safety first.

Why Wise (Formerly TransferWise) is a Game-Changer

- Multi-currency accounts. Local bank details. Hold and spend in 40+ currencies without crazy conversion fees.
- Get bank account numbers in the U.S., U.K., EU, Australia, and more, perfect for getting paid like a local.
- Low-cost transfers. How to use it: Send money between countries for a fraction of what banks charge.

How to use it:

1. Open a Wise account online and verify your identity before you leave.
2. Use it to move money between your U.S. and local bank accounts.
3. Pay bills or rent in your host country without losing 5% to exchange rate games.

Other Banks & Credit Cards Worth Considering for Americans Abroad: Banks:

- Capital One 360 Checking – No foreign transaction fees, easy online access.
- Revolut – Multi-currency accounts, budgeting tools, virtual cards for safer online purchases, and no-fee spending abroad up to certain limits.
- HSBC Premier – Great for global account linking if you need a big-bank presence in multiple countries.
- Citi Global – Worldwide ATMs and decent international service.

Credit Cards:

- Chase Sapphire Preferred/Reserve – No foreign transaction fees, killer travel rewards, and solid travel insurance.

- Capital One Venture – Flexible flights, hotels, or cash back miles.
- American Express Platinum – Airport lounge access, strong travel perks (but not accepted everywhere).
- Bank of America Travel Rewards – No foreign transaction fees, straight-forward rewards.

Tip:

- Always have two debit cards and two credit cards from different banks, in case one gets lost, stolen, or frozen.
- Keep one set in your wallet, the other hidden in your home or luggage.
- Set up account alerts to catch suspicious charges before they drain you dry.
- Banking Abroad Comparison Table

Bank / Card	No Foreign Transaction Fees	ATM Fee Refunds	Multi-Currency Account	Travel Rewards	Best For
Charles Schwab High Yield Investor Checking	✔	✔ (Unlimited)	✘	✘	Everyday withdrawals abroad without fees
Wise Multi-Currency Account	✔	✘ (Low fee per withdrawal)	✔ (40+ currencies)	✘	Getting paid locally & sending low-cost transfers
Capital One 360 Checking	✔	✘	✘	✘	Simple no-fee checking for daily spending
HSBC Premier	✔	✘	✔ (Global account linking)	✘	Moving large sums between countries
Citi Global	✔	✘	✘	✘	ATM access & global branch presence
Chase Sapphire Preferred / Reserve (Credit)	✔	N/A	✘	✔ (High-value travel rewards)	Flights, hotels, & travel insurance
Capital One Venture (Credit)	✔	N/A	✘	✔ (Flexible miles for travel/cash back)	Easy rewards redemption
Amex Platinum (Credit)	✔	N/A	✘	✔ (Lounge access & luxury travel perks)	Frequent flyers who want comfort
Bank of America Travel Rewards (Credit)	✔	N/A	✘	✔ (Simple point system)	Everyday purchases & no FX fees

How to Use This Table

- **Primary Debit Card Abroad:** Charles Schwab or Capital One 360

- **Backup Debit Card:** Wise for transfers, HSBC or Citi for global reach
- **Primary Credit Card Abroad:** Chase Sapphire or Capital One Venture
- **Backup Credit Card:** Bank of America Travel Rewards or Amex Platinum (if accepted where you live)

Pro Move:

Set up autopay on all credit cards from your main U.S. bank account and keep at least one account with a big U.S. bank (Wells Fargo, Chase, BOA) for emergencies, even if you never use it daily.

Step 4: Financial Mindset Shifts for Sustainable Ease

Money isn't just math... It's a mindset.

You can't create freedom from a mindset of fear and scarcity. You must believe you're worthy of ease. You must think you're allowed to be supported.

Here's what we're leaving behind:

- "I have to struggle to earn rest."
- "I can't leave until I'm completely debt-free." "I'm not good with money."
- "I need to wait until I make six figures."

And here's what we're embracing:

- "I can thrive with what I have right now."
- "Rest is my birthright."
- "I am open to new sources of income."
- "Abundance is a vibration, not just a bank balance."

Real Talk: What About Debt?

You don't have to wait until you're debt-free to relocate. Many women move abroad and pay off debt faster because their living expenses are lower.

Here's how:

- Make minimum payments + automate them.
- Choose a country where your U.S. dollar goes further.
- Focus on building income first, then accelerate the payoff.
- se travel rewards or points to minimize flight costs

Pro Tip: If student loans are federal, you may qualify for income-based re-payment that adjusts to your foreign income level. Check out studentaid.gov.

Reflection Prompts:

- What are my current beliefs about money and freedom?
- How much could I save or earn if I made even one small change?
- What income idea excites me most?
- Where is my money being drained, and how can I redirect it?

This isn't about overnight riches. It's about aligned finances that reflect your new life.

You don't need a fortune. You need a plan, a vision, and permission to begin.

Affirmation:

"I release the guilt that says I must suffer to be worthy." "My healing does not require permission or explanation."

Freedom Fund Savings Tracker (Example Layout):

Month	Target Amount	Amount Saved	Notes / Adjustments
January	$500	$450	Unexpected car repair
February	$500	$550	Extra freelance income
March	$500	$500	On track
April	$500	$600	Sold unused furniture
May	$500	$300	Paid annual insurance bill
June	$500	$500	
Total Saved	$3,000	2,900	

Freedom Fund Examples

Here's what saving for your Freedom Fund might look like at different income levels:

- $50,000 salary: Save 25% ($12,500) in 12–18 months by downsizing housing, cutting subscriptions, and focusing on debt payoff.
- $75,000 salary: You can save 30% ($22,500) by combining your primary job with a side hustle and directing all extra income into your fund.
- $100,000 salary: You can save 35% ($35,000) by maintaining your lifestyle and banking the difference.

The amounts differ, but the formula is the same: pick a target, trim expenses, and stack cash with discipline.

Chapter 3: Visas, Paperwork & the FinePrint

Your dream needs legal legs.

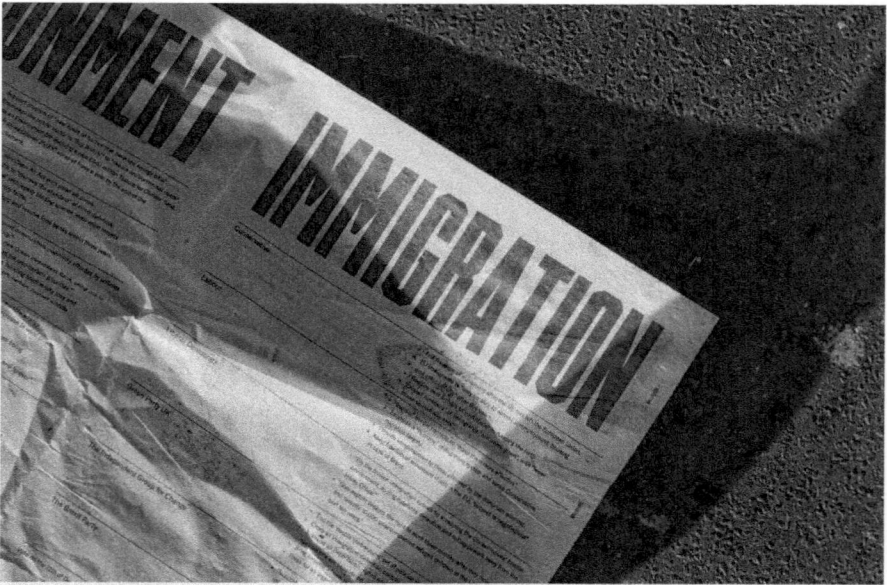

There's nothing sexy about paperwork, but legal status matters if you want your life abroad to be sustainable. You can't just pack your bags and overstay your welcome. In fact, some countries are very strict about immigration, and overstaying your visa can lead to fines, bans, or even detention.

The good news? With the correct information and a little prep, this part doesn't have to be overwhelming. It can even feel empowering, because every document you gather is a declaration: I'm building a life on my terms.

The Most Common Visa Types

Understanding visa types is essential because your visa status determines how long you can stay, what you can do, and whether you're on the right side of the law.

Tourist Visa:

- Usually valid for 30–90 days, depending on the country
- Typically, it doesn't allow you to work. Suitable for "scouting trips" before your big move. Can sometimes be extended, but not always

Retirement Visa:

- Available in many countries for those over a certain age (usually 50+)
- Often requires proof of steady retirement income (pension, Social Security, etc.)
- Countries like Panama, Costa Rica, and Thailand have well-known retirement visa programs.

Digital Nomad Visa:

- Designed for remote workers
- Requires proof of income from outside the country you're moving to
- Often valid for 6–12 months, with renewals available
- Countries offering these visas: Portugal, Croatia, Estonia, Barbados, Mexico, and more

Temporary Residency Visa:

- Allows longer stays, often up to 2 years, sometimes renewable
- May require proof of income or investment
- A stepping stone to permanent residency

Permanent Residency (PR):

- Allows you to stay indefinitely without becoming a citizen
- Usually comes after living in the country for a few years legally.
- May or may not include work privileges, depending on the country

Citizenship or Naturalization:

- The final step, if you plan to stay forever
- Comes with all the rights of a native-born citizen, including voting and sometimes access to local benefits
- Often requires residency, language proficiency, and a clean legal record

Countries with Easy or Flexible Visa Processes

Some countries make it easier than others to relocate. Here are a few that are popular among expats for their flexibility:

Portugal:

- D7 Visa (passive income/retirees)
- Digital Nomad Visa
- Simple path to residency and eventual EU citizenship

Mexico:

- 6-month tourist visa on arrival for many nationalities
- Temporary Resident Visa for retirees or those with income
- No language requirement for residency

Panama:

- Friendly Nations Visa (for citizens of designated countries, including the U.S.)
- Pensionado Visa (for retirees with proof of income)
- Tax-friendly policies for expats

Thailand

Retirement visa for 50+

Education visa (for language learners)

Annual visa renewals, but generally stable for long-term stays

Georgia (the country)

- One-year visa-free stay for many passport holders
- Offers a digital nomad visa
- Low cost of living and tax-friendly

What Documents to Prepare Before You Move

Preparing the proper documents will save you time, stress, and potential delays. Most countries require:

- Valid passport (with at least 6 months remaining)
- Passport-sized photos, Health insurance coverage (some require proof for visa approval)
- Background check (FBI report, often apostilled)
- Birth certificate and/or marriage certificate (apostilled)
- Rental agreement or proof of accommodation, Letter of intent, or application forms specific to the visa type

Pro Tip: Make multiple copies of everything and store them digitally in the cloud (Google Drive, Dropbox, etc.). Also, carry physical copies with you when traveling.

* * *

Apostille Certificates and Document Authentication

Here's the deal: your birth certificate, marriage license, or FBI clearance means nothing abroad until certified. That certification is called an apostille if the country you're moving to is part of the Hague Convention. If not, you'll need a heavier process (authentication + embassy legalization).

Who Needs It

- Anyone applying for a visa, residency, or work permit abroad.
- Families traveling with kids (you'll need children's birth certificates ready).
- Couples using marriage certificates or adoption papers for residency.
- Students or professionals providing diplomas, licenses, or background checks

Why You Need It

- Without it, foreign governments will reject your documents.
- It can save weeks of delays in your visa process.
- If you're not moving immediately, having them ready means you're never stuck waiting on bureaucracy.
- If something happens and you need to leave the U.S. or UK fast, political unrest, family emergency, immigration crackdowns, apostilled documents, or let you apply for a visa or enroll kids in school abroad immediately, without losing time trying to get papers certified while you're under pressure.

How to Get It

U.S. citizens:

- State documents (like birth or marriage certificates) must be obtained through the state Secretary of State's office.
- Go through the U.S. Department of State for federal docs (like FBI background checks).

UK Citizens:

- Apply through the Foreign Office.
- First, you'll need an official certified copy, which you should submit with forms and fees. Processing times vary from a week to a few months.

What to Apostille

- Birth certificates for every family member. Marriage license or divorce decree.
- Children's adoption papers.
- Diplomas, transcripts, and professional licenses
- FBI or police background checks.
- Bank statements, military records, or powers of attorney, if requested by the destination country.

Benefits of Doing It Early

- Apostilled documents are valid worldwide and don't expire.
- Saves you the "why didn't I do this sooner" stress.
- You'll be prepared for sudden opportunities or emergencies.
- If you're forced to leave quickly, you won't have to scramble to prove your identity, your kids' identity, or your legal ties. Everything is already stamped and ready to cross borders.

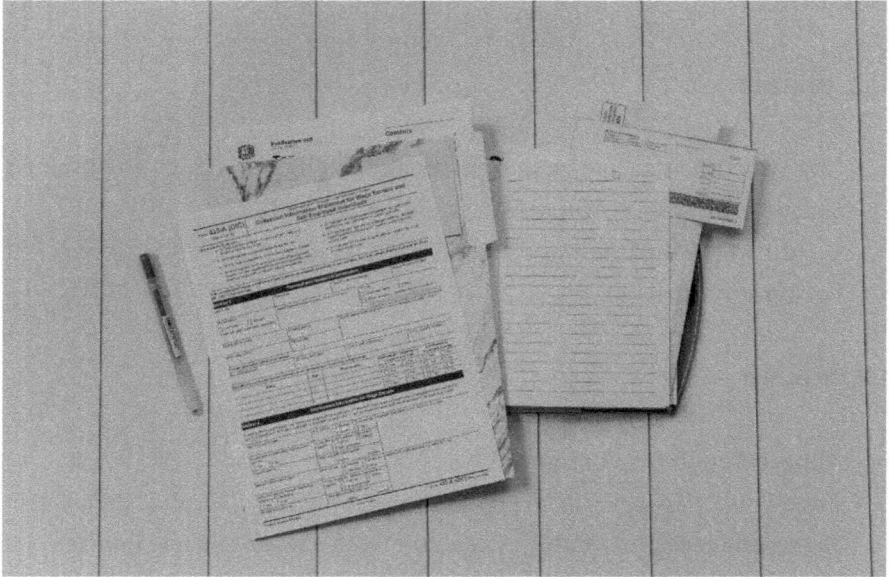

Lesson Learned: Don't Wing Your Residency Process

Let me tell you how I learned this one the complex (and expensive) way. I came over in 2021, thinking I'd feel things out. When I decided to stay for the long haul, I did what most folks would do: I hopped online, looked up the steps for getting my visa, and booked a flight back to the U.S. to handle it.

That meant:

- A round trip to Washington, D.C., Hotel costs
- Visa fees at the consulate
- I returned to my new country and consulted a local immigration pro to start my temporary residency.

Big mistake.

Here's the thing: if I had talked to that immigration pro before booking flights, I would have learned that I could have skipped the trip to D.C. entirely and gone straight into a four-year temporary residency instead of this yearly renewal nonsense I'm stuck with now.

Meanwhile, my husband played it smart—or rather, he played it later. He was still working in the U.S., working three months here and there. When he finally went to my immigration consultant to start his process, he immediately walked out with four years of temporary residency.

Me? I'm still renewing it every year, like clockwork. And yes, I'm salty as hell about it.

The lesson? Don't try to "DIY" your way through immigration just because you think you've done enough Google research. Those online guides don't always tell you the best, fastest, or most cost-effective route for your situation.

Get the pro advice first, then make your moves. It'll save you time and money, and, in my case, a lot of side-eye every time my renewal notice shows up.

Visa Planning Timeline

- 12 months out: Research visa options and eligibility.
- 9 months out: Gather financial records, transcripts, and medical paperwork.
- 6 months out: Begin the application process for long-stay visas.
- 3 months out: Submit applications, schedule embassy appointments, and pay fees.
- One month out: Confirm approval, finalize travel, and prepare arrival documents.

Top 5 Mistakes in Visa Applications

1. Starting Too Late - Processing times can be months. Begin at least 6−9 months ahead.
2. Relying Only on Google - Immigration websites change often; confirm with an official consulate or immigration lawyer.
3. Incomplete Documentation - Missing one document can reset your timeline. Triple-check your tourist visa checklist.
4. Choosing the Wrong Visa: A tourist visa might be quick, but it cannot be converted to residency in some countries.
5. Ignoring Renewal Rules - Some visas require renewal within a narrow window—miss it, and you start over.

* * *

How to Apply for a Long-Term Visa to Move Abroad

Step 1: Research your destination and visa requirements

Start by picking the country you want to move to and visiting its official immigration or consulate website. These sites will tell you if you need a visa for stays over 90 days (most do) and what types of visas they offer. Look up the visa categories (work, study, family, retirement, etc.) and who is eligible for each. For example, many nationals can visit Canada visa-free on an electronic travel authorization (eTA) for up to 90 days. Still, any more extended stay (to work or settle) requires a formal visa. Note the key requirements − passport validity (usually 6 months past your stay), financial proof, and health or background checks. Keep a checklist of all conditions and documents mentioned on the official site.

Next, compare the rules for your nationality. Immigration policies vary worldwide: Canada, for example, publishes multiple visa classes (Temporary Resident, Work, Study, Permanent Resident, etc.). In Europe's Schengen Area (e.g., Germany, France), U.S. or EU citizens may enter visa-free for 90 days, but longer stays require a national long-stay visa or residence permit. Find out if your country of choice has any special visas (like retiree or digital-nomad programs) and note the fees and processing times. In all cases, rely on official government sources (embassy/immigration websites) for the most current rules.

Step 2: Determine your visa category and eligibility.

Decide why you're moving and pick the matching visa type. Different purposes have different rules: student visas require school enrollment and proof of tuition, work visas usually need a job offer or sponsorship, family visas need documented relationships, etc. Ensure you meet that category's eligibility criteria (age, education, job skills, income, language ability, etc.). For example, skilled worker visas often use a points system, while a retirement visa may require proof of sufficient income or savings. If you have multiple options, compare them to see which is easiest and whether it leads to permanent residency. Remember that some visas (like tourist or business visas) cannot be converted to residency; in that case, you'll need to leave and reapply.

Step 3: Gather all required documents.

Every visa application requires thorough documentation. Typical items include: your passport (valid well beyond your stay – usually 6+ months), recent passport-style photos, and any pre-filled application forms (online confirmation or printed). You'll also need a payment receipt for the visa fee. Beyond that, assemble all supporting papers: financial statements or bank letters, employment or admission letters, proof of residence (like a lease or invitation), and any country-specific items (e.g., police clearance, medical exam). Original documents are usually required for the interview, so make copies of everything just in case. Consult the embassy's checklist (often provided online) to ensure you have every item; your application can be delayed or rejected if something is missing.

Step 4: Complete the application and pay fees.

Fill out the official visa application form carefully. Many countries now use online portals. For example, Germany offers a Consular Services Portal where you submit your data and documents electronically before visiting the embassy. If the country uses paper forms, download them from the embassy website or pick them up from the consulate. Pay the visa application fee (it's usually non-refundable). You may pay online or at a bank as instructed. Keep your fee receipt: you will need its number
for your appointment.

In short:

- Please fill out the visa form (online or print) and check it thoroughly.
- Pay the visa application fee and save the proof of payment.
- Print or download confirmation pages (if online) and any barcodes/appointment letters.

Step 5: Schedule and attend your interview/biometric appointment.
After submitting the form and paying, you'll usually need an in-person appointment. Schedule it through the embassy's online system. You'll typically need your passport number, application confirmation, and fee receipt to book the date. You should apply and interview at the embassy or consulate of your home country (some places don't accept out-of-home applications). Wait times can be long, so book as early as you can. On the day of your appointment, bring all required documents: your passport, the printed application or DS-160 confirmation page, the fee payment receipt, one or more passport photos, and any supporting documents you gathered.

You will likely submit fingerprints or biometrics at this visit. The consular officer will interview you to verify your information and intent. Be honest and concise: they want to confirm your travel purpose and ties back home.

Step 6: Visa processing and receiving your visa.

After the interview, the consulate will process your application. If approved, you will pay any additional issuance fee (depending on nationality), and then your passport with the visa stamp will be returned to you, often via courier. The U.S. process, "depending on nationality, you may need to pay a visa issuance fee... [then] the embassy will explain how your passport with visa will be returned". When you get your passport back, check the visa immediately: verify that your name is correct, the visa type and dates are right, and note how long you can stay. The visa only permits you to travel to the country's border; the final entry decision happens at immigration on arrival. Plan your travel (flight, shipping belongings, etc.) after you have the visa.

Step 7: Arrive and register in your new country.

Once you arrive, present your passport and visa at immigration control. You will receive an entry stamp or form allowing you to stay temporarily. Follow local registration rules: Many countries require new arrivals to register their address or residence. For example, in Germany, you must register (Anmeldung) with the local city office within two weeks and apply for a residence permit at the immigration office within

90 days. Similarly, long-stay visa holders in Spain or France often need to obtain a residence card after arrival. Ensure you know the deadlines: A long-stay visa typically leads to a residence permit that may need annual renewal. Also, as required, arrange local necessities (like health insurance, tax IDs, and a bank account). Carry your residence permit or registration papers with you and comply with the conditions of your visa (for example, don't work if your visa doesn't allow it).

Step 8: Transition to permanent residency (if desired).

If you plan to settle indefinitely, learn the path to permanent residency. Most countries allow you to apply for permanent status only after you have lived there legally for some years. The requirements vary: You may need to submit additional applications, prove continuous residence, stable income, language ability, and good conduct. Check the immigration department's website for instructions on "permanent residency" or "settlement" in your country. For example, Canada's Express Entry system is a well-defined route to permanent residency, while many European countries require five or more years of residence and a language exam. Keep your temporary status valid until you secure permanent status. Once granted, permanent residency usually confers the right to live and work indefinitely (though it may still require occasional renewals).

Summary:

Moving abroad long-term is a multi-step process. In brief: **(1)** Research the official visa rules for your destination ; **(2)** Choose the right visa category for your purpose ; **(3)** Gather all required documents documents and ensure your passport is valid ; **(4)** Apply online or at the consulate and pay fees ; **(5)** Attend your visa appointment with all paperwork ; **(6)** Receive the visa and check it carefully ; **(7)** Enter and register in the new country (e.g., obtain a residence permit); and **(8)** Fulfill any requirements if you later seek permanent residency. At each step, use official immigration resources and follow instructions closely – this "hand-holding" approach will help ensure a smooth start to your new life abroad.

**The complete Step-by-Step Visa Guide, with checklists and expanded instructions, is in the companion workbook.

Reminder: Visa planning is like building a bridge; skip a step, and you might swim. Follow the process in order, and you'll walk across with dry feet and peace of mind.

* * *

Quick Visa Tips

Save yourself the stress, money, and "why didn't I do this sooner" moments.

Talk to an Immigration Pro First

- Book a consultation before booking flights or submitting applications.
- Ask about all possible visa types you qualify for.

Map Out the Costs Upfront

- Include flights, hotels (if travel to a consulate is required), application fees, translations, apostilles, and legal help.
- Factor in renewal costs, and they add up.

Plan for the Longest Validity You Can Get

- Ask if you can apply directly for a multi-year residency.
- Weigh the cost now versus renewing every year.

Understand the Renewal Timeline

- Some countries only give you a short renewal window.
- Set reminders well in advance so you're never scrambling

Keep Every Document Digital + Physical

- Cloud storage for copies (Google Drive, Dropbox)

- A physical folder for originals when you travel or go to immigration.

Don't Assume Online Info is the Whole Truth

- Country rules change
- Immigration pros are on the ground and know the latest updates.

Reminder: Residency is not just paperwork, it's your permission to stay. Treat it like gold, because your dream life abroad is a long vacation without it.

* * *

Working with Immigration Pros vs. DIY

Can you file your own visa paperwork? Yes. Should you? That depends.

DIY Pros:

- Saves money
- Can work well for simple visas (tourist, digital nomad)
- Helps you understand the process deeply

DIY Cons:

- High chance of errors or missing documents
- Language barriers on official websites
- Delays or rejections due to technical mistakes

Hiring an Immigration Professional:

- Ideal for more complex processes like permanent residency or citizenship
- Helps you avoid costly mistakes. Speeds up the process in many cases
- Often includes translation, appointment scheduling, and legal advice

Red Flag: Be wary of people who promise "guaranteed" approvals. Always verify credentials and ask for references.

Immigration Attorneys and Paperwork You Need to Know

Moving abroad isn't only about packing a suitcase. It's paperwork. It's proof. It's ensuring your documents hold weight outside the U.S. or UK borders. Too many people skip this part and end up stuck. Don't do that to yourself. This section is here so you don't get blindsided.

Immigration Attorneys Who Handle Global Relocation

If you want professional help, these trusted firms know how to move UK citizens to countries worldwide. Some even have culturally aware services for Black families.

- **Law Office of Alfonso Venegas, PLLC (USA)** – Texas-based, with expertise in moving Americans to Spain and Mexico. Specializes in non-lucrative visas. Website: venegaslawfirm.com
- **Diaspora Law (USA)** – Licensed in all 50 states. Handles family and business immigration cases globally. Website: diasporalaw.com
- **Immigration Advice Service (UK/USA)** – UK-headquartered, with U.S. offices. Helps U.S. and UK citizens emigrate worldwide. Website: iasservices.org.uk
- **Total Law International (UUK** – Global team handling visas for the U.S., UK, Canada, Spain, and Ireland. Website: total.law
- **Withers (International)** – Big international firm with U.S., UK, UUK, EU, and
- Asia offices. Handles high-level relocations. Website: withersworld-wide.com

- **Muldoon Britton (USA)** – New York–based, specializes in helping AmericaUUK visasUKvisas (student, skilled worker, family). Website: muldoonbrittonus.com

Tip: If you don't like these, check AILA (American Immigration Lawyers Association) or
UK's OISCISC directory for licensed immigration attorneys.

U.S. Passports: Book and Card

Too many people only think about a passport when buying a flight. That's a mistake. In today's climate, especially with immigration crackdowns, you need one ready.

Who Needs It

- Every U.S. citizen traveling abroad, period.
- Families traveling with children (even babies need a passport.
- People living near borders or traveling often to Canada, Mexico, or the Caribbean should also get the passport card.

Why You Need It

- The passport book is required for international air travel.
- The passport card is optional but cheap, wallet-sized, and works for land and sea travel between the U.S., Canada, Mexico, Bermuda, and the Caribbean.
- Government-issued IDs prove citizenship and are proper during domestic flights, checkpoints, or immigration sweeps.

How to Get It

- Apply at travel.state.gov or at a U.S. post office acceptance center.

- Use form DS-11 (first time) or DS-82 (renewal).
- You'll need proof of citizenship (birth certificate or naturalization certificate), a photo, and fees.
- Processing takes weeks unless you pay for expedited service.
- You can apply for both the book and the card simultaneously.

Benefits of Having Both

Book: Full access to every international destination.
   Card: Handy backup ID and quicker crossings at land/sea borders.
   Together: You're covered for emergencies, faster travel, and everyday proof of citizenship.

* * *

The Truth About Dual Citizenship and Second Passports

Dual citizenship means you hold legal citizenship in two countries. It can offer tremendous benefits like:

- Visa-free travel to more countries
- The right to live, work, and own property in both nations
- Access to healthcare, education, and social benefits

But it also comes with responsibilities:

- You may need to file taxes in both countries.
- Not all countries allow dual citizenship (e.g., Japan and India generally do not)
- U.S. citizens remain subject to U.S. tax law regardless of residence

Second passports can be acquired through:

- Naturalization (after years of residency)
- Descent (if you have parents/grandparents from another country)
- Investment (some countries offer "citizenship by investment" programs)

Countries known for easier dual citizenship pathways:

- Ireland (if you have Irish ancestry)
- Italy (via bloodline or long-term residency)
- Dominica, St. Kitts & Nevis (via investment)
- Portugal (after five years of legal residency)

Reflection Prompts:

- Which visa path best suits my situation right now?
- How long am I planning to stay in my new country?
- Am I more drawn to temporary freedom or permanent roots?
- What legal or logistical detail do I need to start researching this week?
- Freedom abroad starts with legal clarity. The paperwork may be tedious, but it's the price of peace, safety, and sovereignty.

And you, my friend, are worth the effort.

Affirmation:
"I don't need to know everything to take the first step."
"My spirit will recognize where I am meant to land."

Chapter 4: Top Countries to Consider (And Why)

There is no perfect country. But there is an ideal fit for you.

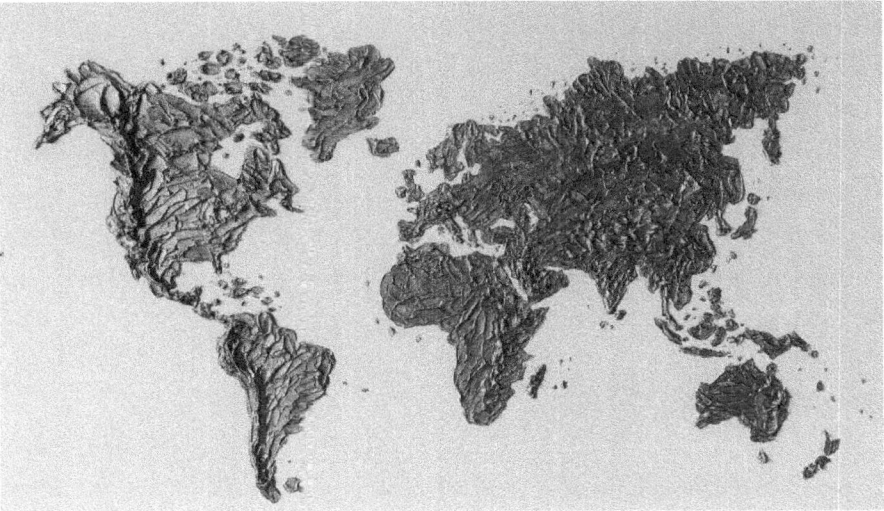

Every destination has its own rhythm of safety, cost, culture, healthcare and community. Below, we spotlight countries that excel in making expats—especially Black and LGBTQ+ travelers—feel welcomed, empowered, and safe. We'll look beyond the beach pictures and explore real-life factors affecting your quality of life abroad.

Your Nearby Escape Hatches

Listen up. You're not alone if you feel like the American dream is a bit of a bait-and-switch. The hunt for a better quality of life pushes more people to look beyond the border. The good news? You don't have to sail to the other side of the world to find it. Two of your best options are right next door.

Let's cut the fluff and get into it.

Canada

Canada consistently ranks high for quality of life, safety, and healthcare. It's stable, clean, and close to home, making visits back to see family straightforward.

How you get in:
   One of the most straightforward paths is the Express Entry program. It's a points-based system that scores you on your age, education, work experience, and language skills. If your score is high enough, you get permanent residency. Budget around $1,525 for the processing and right-of-permanent-residence fees.

The reality check:

Forget the idea that you'll land a perfect job immediately. Canada's job market is competitive, full stop. Many employers want to see a permanent local address or a Canadian bank account, which means you'll likely have to move first and then find work. Patience isn't just a virtue here; it's a requirement.

* * *

México

Look south if your soul needs sun and your wallet needs a break. México offers a seriously low cost of living. A couple can live well on less than $2,300 a month, including a decent place to live and access to incredible beach communities. The warm weather is just the cherry on top.

How you get in:

México is one of the easiest places for Americans to get long-term residency worldwide. To stay beyond the 180-day tourist visa, apply for the Residente Temporal program. This is a one-year, renewable visa. The key is proving you can support yourself. You'll need to show about $62,000 in investments or bank accounts over the past year and a steady monthly income of at least $3,700.

This visa is a solid pathway to permanent residency or even citizenship. And if you have your eye on a beachfront property, know that as a foreigner, you'll need to set up a real estate trust, called a fideicomiso. It's a one-time fee of around $2,000, plus a few hundred in annual charges. Just factor it into your budget.

The reality check:

Stop watching the news and thinking the whole country is a warzone. There are dangerous areas, but the popular expat and tourist hubs are generally safe. Use your head. Don't flash cash, be aware of your surroundings, and avoid remote areas you don't know. Basic street smarts are all you need to live a peaceful life there. Stop just thinking about it.

It's time to match that energy with action. If you can go, then go

* * *

Best for Families

Portugal: Europe's Warm-Hearted Gem

Safety: Low crime rates; ranked among the safest countries in Europe. **Cost of Living:** Moderate, $1,500–$2,500/month for a comfortable lifestyle. **Cultural Welcome:** English is widely spoken; Portuguese hospitality shines in Lisbon, Porto, and the Algarve. **Healthcare:** Universal public system complemented by private options; high standards at low cost. **Community:** Thriving digital nomad scene; growing Afro-Caribbean and LGBTQ+ networks. **Why It Fits:** Offers EU access, renewable visas (D7, Golden Visa), and a blend of

Old World charm with modern amenities.

Cultural Insight for Black Women:

- Portugal has far less overt anti-Blackness than the U.S., though subtle bias may exist.
- Hair and skin care products are increasingly available, especially in Lisbon.
- Police generally do not target Black expats, and you are more likely to be treated as a visitor than a threat.
- Black women report being treated with curiosity, not hostility, particularly when not mistaken for immigrants from Africa.

* * *

Costa Rica: Pura Vida and Peace of Mind

Safety: One of the safest countries in Central America; no standing army.

Cost of Living: $1,500–$2,500/month, with retiree-specific discounts on utilities and services. **Cultural Welcome:** Casual, eco-conscious culture; Spanish is primary, but English is used daily in tourist areas. **Healthcare:** Universal public system (Caja) plus private plans; known for medical tourism. **Community:** Expat enclaves in Atenas, Grecia, and coastal towns; inclusive LGBTQ+ scene. **Why It Fits:** Retirement (pensionado) visa for passive income, abundant nature, and emphasis on wellness.

Cultural Insight for Black Women:

- Afro-Costa Rican communities exist on the Caribbean coast; they are generally very welcoming.
- Some colorism exists, but racial bias is less institutionalized than in the U.S.
- Hair and skin care options are limited outside major cities — plan.
- You're seen as a peaceful tourist or expat, not a threat.

* * *

México: Close-Knit Culture, Close to Home

Safety: Varies by region; research local conditions, citiesMéridaMérida, Oaxaca, and Guanajuato are consistently safe. **Cost of Living:** $1,000–$2,000/month in most expat-friendly cities. Cultural **Welcome:** Warm, family-oriented culture with deep indigenous and Afro-Mexican roots. **Healthcare:** Both private and public systems are available; private care is affordable and high quality. **Community:** Robust Black, Indigenous, and LGBTQ+ circles; numerous meetups and online groups. **Why It Fits:** Proximity to the U.S., flexible residency (temporary resident visa), and vibrant arts and food scenes.

Cultural Insight for Black Women:

- Anti-Blackness exists but is less institutional; most tension is directed toward Indigenous groups.
- Afro-Mexican visibility is increasing. Black expats report curiosity but rarely hostility.
- Natural hair is celebrated in expat circles; braiders, stylists,

- Black-owned salons are found in major cities.
- Police interactions can vary; know your visa rights and carry proper ID.

* * *

Best for Retirees

Panama: Modern Comfort, Tropical Clime

Safety: Generally safe in expat areas; stay aware in urban centers. **Cost of Living:** $1,500–$2,500/month; housing and utilities similar to mid-range U.S. cities. **Cultural Welcome:** English is widely spoken in business and expat zones; there is a strong American cultural influence. **Healthcare:** Top private hospitals in Panama City; cheap but reliable public options. **Community:** Panamanian retirees program (pensionado), Friendly Nations Visa, diverse expat circles. **Why It Fits:** Dollar-based economy, direct flights to major U.S. hubs, modern infrastructure.

Cultural Insight for Black Women:

· Panama has a large Afro-Caribbean and Afro-Latinx population; you won't feel "othered."
· English-speaking locals ease the transition.
· Black expats say they feel safer and more respected than in the U.S.
· Hair products are available in urban areas; wellness spaces are growing.

* * *

Cuenca, Ecuador

Safety: Cuenca is considered one of the safest cities in Ecuador, especially in expat-heavy neighborhoods. Petty theft can occur, so stay alert in crowded markets. **Cost of Living:** $1,200–$1,800/month covers rent, food, and healthcare for a comfortable lifestyle. Apartments in the historic district or near El Centro range from $400–$700/month. **Cultural Welcome:** Spanish is the primary language. English is spoken in expat zones but not widely elsewhere, so learning basic Spanish is helpful. Locals are warm toward expats, especially families and retirees. **Healthcare:** High-quality private clinics with low costs. Routine doctor visits average $30–$40. Many expats praise the affordability of dental and vision care. **Community:** Active retiree and digital nomad circles, plus affordable Pensioner Visa ($800/month income requirement). The African diaspora is growing in presence through cultural exchange and art communities. **Why It Fits:** Mild year-round climate, walkable historic city, UNESCO World Heritage charm, and affordable retirement or long-term stay options.

Cultural Insight for Black Women:

- Black women report being received warmly, though Afro-Ecuadorian culture is more visible along the coast than in Cuenca.
- You may often be asked about your background, seen more as curiosity than hostility.
- There is growing interest in African American culture, primarily through music, natural hair, and style.

* * *

Brazil

Safety: Safety varies widely. Expat-friendly cities like Florianópolis, Curitiba, or specific neighborhoods in São Paulo and Rio offer safer living. Petty theft is common in tourist hubs; violent crime occurs in marginalized areas. Awareness and choosing the right neighborhood are key. **Cost of Living:** $1,500–$2,500/month provides a middle-class lifestyle. Rent in São Paulo's expat-friendly neighborhoods ranges from $500–$1,200/month. Cheaper in smaller coastal cities. **Cultural Welcome:** Brazil has the largest African-descended population outside of Africa, making it one of the most racially diverse countries in the world. Portuguese is the official language; English is spoken sparingly outside business and expat groups. **Healthcare: The** Public healthcare system (SUS) is free but often crowded. Many expats opt for private insurance, which is affordable compared to the U.S. Major cities like São Paulo have world-class hospitals. **Community:** Vibrant Black expat networks, plus strong local Afro-Brazilian cultural hubs in Salvador, Rio, and São Paulo. Immigration options include retirement and digital nomad visas (proof of ~$1,500/month income). Why **ItFits:** Rich cultural scene, deep African heritage, vibrant music and food, and affordable healthcare compared to the U.S., an excellent option for retirees, creatives, and digital workers who want both affordability and cultural richness.

Cultural Insight for Black Women:

- Brazil can feel affirming because of the sheer presence and visibility of Afro-descended culture, food, music, religion, and fashion.
- In Salvador, especially, Black women often feel celebrated. That said, racial inequality still exists, with class and colorism shaping experiences.
- Many Black expats enjoy blending into the cultural landscape while contributing to a global conversation about Black identity.

* * *

Best for Low Cost of Living

Thailand

Cultural Relevance: Rich traditions in food, art, and festivals, with hubs that welcome foreigners.

- **Language:** Thai is key for deeper connections, though English is used daily in cities.
- **Black Expat Presence**: Moderate, centered in Bangkok, Chiang Mai, and Phuket.
- **Cost of Living:** ~$800–$1,300/month.

* * *

Vietnam

- **Cultural Relevance:** Strong traditions in food, festivals, and community life, with rising tourism.
- **Language:** Vietnamese is essential outside major cities, and English is used daily in expat hubs.
- **Black Expat Presence:** Small but active, mainly teachers and entrepreneurs in Ho Chi Minh City and Hanoi.
- **Cost of Living:** ~$700–$1,100/month

* * *

Georgia (Tbilisi)

Safety: Tbilisi is generally safe and has low violent crime rates. Petty theft can happen in crowded tourist areas. Police presence is strong in city centers, and locals are protective of foreigners. **Cost of Living:** $1,200–$1,800/month covers rent, utilities, food and healthcare. A one-bedroom apartment in the city center averages $400–$700/month, cheaper outside the center. Daily expenses like fresh produce and transportation are very affordable. **Cultural Welcome:** Georgian hospitality is legendary. Locals are warm and curious about foreigners, especially Americans. English is spoken by younger generations and in business, but Russian and Georgian dominate. Learning a few phrases of Georgian earns you respect. **Healthcare:** Public healthcare is improving, but it is limited. Most expats use private clinics, which are affordable and staffed with Western-trained doctors. Routine visits run $30–$50, and dental care is inexpensive. **Community:** Georgia offers one of the most flexible residency paths for expats. U.S. passport holders can stay visa-free for a year, renewable by a simple border crossing. A growing digital nomad and entrepreneur scene thrives in Tbilisi, supported by co-working hubs and tech-friendly policies. **Why It Fits:** One-year visa-free stay, affordable cost of living, breathtaking mountain scenery, rich food and wine culture, and strategic location between Europe and Asia, it's desirable for digital nomads and retirees who want affordability with strong cultural roots.

Cultural Insight for Black Women:

- Georgia has a small Black expat community, so visibility is high.
- Most encounters are rooted in curiosity rather than hostility, though stares are common outside cosmopolitan areas. Many
- Black women report feeling safe but highly noticeable. Locals admire African American culture, particularly music, style, and resilience.
- Building community may take effort, but expats who engage in local traditions, wine festivals, dance, and food gatherings are warmly embraced.

* * *

Best for LGBTQ+ Community

The Netherlands (Amsterdam, Rotterdam, Utrecht

Legal Protections

The Netherlands was the first country to legalize same-sex marriage in 2001. LGBTQ couples have full equality under Dutch law, including joint adoption, surrogacy, inheritance rights, and strong anti-discrimination protections. Residency sponsorship for partners is straightforward.

Safety

Dutch cities rank high for safety and public trust in police. Hate crimes are rare but not absent. The Netherlands has clear legal consequences for harassment or violence.

Cost of Living

Housing is higher in Amsterdam but moderate in cities like Rotterdam or Utrecht. Groceries and public transport are more affordable than in London or Paris.

Healthcare

Universal healthcare is excellent. Expats must buy Dutch health insurance within four months of arrival, but services are reliable and accessible.

Community

Amsterdam's Pride and queer nightlife are world-renowned. Rotterdam and Utrecht offer smaller but active scenes. Black LGBTQ expats find support in multicultural neighborhoods, though some report subtle bias.

Cultural Insights

Dutch society is famously liberal and direct. People are open-minded but value privacy. Learning basic Dutch helps with local integration, though many speak English.

* * *

Spain (Madrid, Barcelona, Valencia)

Legal Protections

Same-sex marriage has been legal since 2005. Spain ranks among the top 5 LGBTQ-friendly countries in Europe. Full rights include adoption, parental recognition, inheritance, and equal protection in domestic violence cases.

Safety

Spain is considered safe, though pickpocketing is common in big cities. LGBTQ-targeted violence is rare but can occur in smaller conservative areas.

Cost of Living

Madrid and Barcelona are more expensive but still cheaper than London or Paris. Valencia and smaller cities are much more affordable, with 30–40% lower rents.

Healthcare

Spain's public healthcare is highly rated, affordable, and covers LGBTQ-specific needs, including gender-affirming care.

Community

Madrid hosts one of the largest Pride celebrations in the world. Barcelona's LGBTQ nightlife is lively year-round. Smaller coastal cities have growing, welcoming expat scenes. Black LGBTQ expats report mixed experiences: while many enjoy strong acceptance, occasional racial stereotyping exists.

Cultural Insights

Spaniards value socializing, food, and family life. The Mediterranean pace is slower than that of Northern Europe. English is widely spoken in tourist areas, but learning Spanish is key for deeper integration.

* * *

Canada (Toronto, Vancouver, Montréal

Legal Protections

Canada has had nationwide marriage equality since 2005, backed by the 1982 Charter of Rights and Freedoms. LGBTQ people enjoy equal family rights, tax benefits, surrogacy, and adoption. Transgender people have the right to self-identify without surgery.

Safety

Canada ranks among the safest countries in the world. LGBTQ-targeted violence is rare, but urban areas experience occasional incidents. Hate crimes are prosecuted under federal law.

Cost of Living

Toronto and Vancouver are costly (housing, groceries). Montréal, Ottawa, and Halifax are more affordable and still very diverse.

Healthcare

Canada's public healthcare system (varies by province) ensures essential medical services; many LGBTQ+ inclusive services are available in large cities. Access to specialized or transition-related care often depends on provincial policy, wait times, and provider availability. As with any country, moving entirely into a new health system (if relocating) requires checking regional/prior-residency entitlements and private-supplement options.

Community

Universal healthcare is free for citizens and permanent residents. Most provinces include gender-affirming care. Private insurance is needed for some expats during residency processing.

Cultural Insights

Canada is multicultural and progressive. Although winter weather can be extreme, social integration is easier due to the country's openness. Activism is visible, and many Black LGBTQ voices lead local movements.

* * *

Belgium (Brussels, Antwerp, Ghent)

Legal Protections

Belgium has legalized same-sex marriage since 2003. It is ranked among the top European countries for LGBTQ+ rights — for example, in 2024, it achieved a very high position on the ILGA-Europe Rainbow Map. Full rights include adoption, parental recognition, inheritance rights, and protection from discrimination.

Safety

Belgium is generally considered safe for LGBTQ+ people. Big cities like Brussels, Antwerp, and Ghent have well-established queer communities and visible Pride events. However, caution is still wise in less urban or more conservative areas, as in many places.

Cost of Living

Cities like Brussels and Antwerp are among the most expensive in Belgium, especially for housing, though they generally still have lower costs than major global hubs like London or Paris. Smaller cities like Ghent tend to be more affordable.

Healthcare

Belgium has high-quality public healthcare; transgender and gender-affirming care is available, although navigating the system may take some time.

Community

Brussels hosts major LGBTQ+ events (for example, its Pride). Antwerp and Ghent also have lively scenes. Belgium's progressive legal framework helps foster inclusive spaces.

Cultural Insights

Belgians value socializing (often around cafés, beer culture, and outdoor terraces), and there is a blend of Flemish and French-speaking influences (and more in Brussels). Learning some Dutch (Flemish) or French will help deeper integration, even though English is widely spoken in urban areas.

* * *

Malta (Valletta, St. Julian's, Sliema)

Legal Protections

Malta is often cited as the most progressive country in Europe for LGBTQ+ rights. Same-sex marriage has been legal since 2017. Comprehensive protections exist, including gender self-determination and a ban on conversion therapy.

Safety

Malta is generally very safe for LGBTQ+ people. The island has a strong reputation for inclusion, especially in tourist-friendly areas like St.Julian's and Sliema.

Cost of Living

Living on the islands can be more expensive than some mainland European locations, especially in more tourist- or expat-oriented areas (sea-front Sliema, St.Julian's). Valletta is historic and charming, but housing can be premium.

Healthcare

Public healthcare is available; Malta also provides gender identity protections and services.

Community

Malta's Pride and LGBTQ+ community life are vibrant. The island lifestyle, tourism, and Mediterranean climate make it a popular location for queer travelers and residents.

Cultural Insights

The Maltese are friendly, family-oriented, and the pace is more relaxed than in major cities. English is widely spoken (alongside Maltese). Being part of the local social scene often helps with integration.

* * *

Portugal (Lisbon, Porto)

Legal Protections

Same-sex marriage has been legal in Portugal since June 5,2010. Adoption by same-sex couples has also been permitted since 2016. Discrimination protections exist, although some rights advocacy groups note gaps remain.

Safety
Portugal is considered reasonably safe and LGBTQ+ friendly, particularly in bigger cities like Lisbon and Porto, though local norms always vary.

Cost of Living
Lisbon and Porto are more affordable than many Western European capitals, although costs in the city centre are rising. Smaller Portuguese cities are significantly cheaper.

Healthcare

Portugal's national health service provides good coverage; LGBTQ+ specific needs are increasingly recognized, though waiting times may apply.

Community
Lisbon has a lively LGBTQ+ scene with bars, clubs, and annual Pride events. Porto also has a growing queer community.

Cultural Insights
Portuguese culture values socializing, food, and a relaxed pace. English is spoken every day in tourist zones, but learning Portuguese will deepen integration and local connection.

* * *

Taiwan (Taipei, Taichung, Kaohsiung)

Legal Protections

Taiwan became the first place in Asia to legalise same-sex marriage (May 24,2019). Married same-sex couples have most rights of opposite-sex couples, including inheritance and property rights. However, some gaps remain (e.g., joint adoption of non-biological children).

Safety

Taipei is highly LGBTQ+ friendly, with a visible queer nightlife. Taiwan is comparatively open in the region, though caution may still be prudent in more rural or conservative areas.

Cost of Living

Taipei is one of the more expensive places in Taiwan, but the overall cost of living is moderate compared to major Western cities. Taichung and Kaohsiung tend to be more affordable.

Healthcare

Taiwan's healthcare system is robust and accessible; gender-affirming services are increasingly available, though local practices and wait times vary.

Community

Taipei hosts significant Pride events and has a strong queer community

Taichung and Kaohsiung increasingly offer inclusive spaces, though on a smaller scale..

Cultural Insights

Taiwanese culture blends modernity with tradition. Mandarin is dominant; English is less common outside tourist areas, so learning some Mandarin will help. The pace is relatively relaxed compared to mega-metros elsewhere.

* * *

Thailand (Bangkok, Chiang Mai, Phuket)

Legal Protections

Thailand does not yet have nationwide marriage equality. Still, in 2025, lawmakers passed a same-sex civil partnership bill that grants many of the same legal rights as marriage, including inheritance, hospital visitation, and shared property. Full marriage equality is expected to follow soon. Transgender people can legally change their name, but still face legal and bureaucratic barriers when it comes to gender marker changes on official documents.

Safety

Thailand is generally safe for LGBTQ individuals, especially in major cities like Bangkok, Chiang Mai, and Phuket, which are known for their visible and vibrant queer communities. While public displays of affection may draw attention, especially in rural areas, violence against LGBTQ people is rare. Anti-discrimination laws exist in limited areas but are not always enforced.

Cost of Living

Bangkok is the most expensive city in Thailand, particularly in central and expat-heavy neighborhoods. Chiang Mai and Phuket are more affordable, offering a lower cost of living while still providing access to queer-friendly spaces, healthcare, and lifestyle amenities.

Healthcare

Thailand offers high-quality healthcare at relatively low cost. Bangkok and Chiang Mai are home to internationally accredited hospitals, and gender-affirming surgery is world-renowned and widely accessible. Public healthcare doesn't typically cover transition-related care for foreigners, but private insurance and medical tourism options are popular among expats and trans individuals.

Community

Thailand has a strong LGBTQ community, especially in urban centers. Bangkok boasts numerous gay bars, saunas, drag shows, and annual Pride celebrations. Chiang Mai and Phuket also have growing LGBTQ networks. While not all locals are fully accepting, social tolerance is generally high, and queer people are often visible in entertainment and public life.

Cultural Insights

Thai society values politeness and discretion, which shape public expressions of identity. The concept of "kathoey" (commonly referred to as ladyboys) has long been part of the culture, though true equality for all LGBTQ identities is still a work in progress. Expats often find integration relatively easy, especially in progressive, tourist-friendly areas.

* * *

South Africa (Cape Town, Johannesburg)

Legal Protections

South Africa stands out in Africa: discrimination on sexual orientation is prohibited under the constitution, and same-sex marriage has been legal since 2006. Adoption by same-sex couples and other rights are available.

Safety

In major urban centres like Cape Town and Johannesburg, LGBTQ+ travelers and residents generally find welcoming spaces, especially in known queer neighborhoods. However, outside those zones and particularly in some townships or rural settings, there remains a risk of homophobic violence and discrimination.

Cost of Living

Living in Cape Town or Johannesburg can vary widely: city centres or coast-fronts cost more, while suburbs and certain townships are more affordable.

Healthcare

South Africa's public and private healthcare system covers many needs; some urban clinics and NGOs specialise in LGBTQ+ health.

Community

Cape Town has one of the most developed queer scenes in Africa, especially in areas like Green Point. Johannesburg likewise has vibrant pride events and LGBTQ+ hubs. But underlying social challenges persist.

Cultural Insights

South Africa's society is diverse in language, culture, and attitudes. While the legal framework is strong, social acceptance is uneven. Traveling and living openly in urban, more progressive neighborhoods is feasible; awareness and sensitivity are advised in less urban or more conservative regions.

* * *

Argentina (Buenos Aires, Córdoba, Mendoza)

Legal Protections

Argentina was the first country in Latin America to legalise same-sex marriage nationwide (in July 2010). Full adoption rights for same-sex couples are recognized.

Safety

BuenosAires has an intense queer scene with visible LGBTQ+ life; Córdoba and Mendoza also offer welcoming spaces, though the scene is smaller. Social acceptance is generally good in urban areas, but disparities exist especially in more rural or conservative regions.

Cost of Living

Argentina's cost of living is relatively moderate compared to many Western countries, though inflation and economic fluctuations affect affordability. Major cities will cost more than regional provinces.

Healthcare

Argentinian public healthcare covers a broad spectrum of services; gender-affirming care is available, particularly in BuenosAires.

Community

BuenosAires hosts one of the biggest Pride celebrations in Latin America; queer culture is vibrant. Córdoba and Mendoza are more relaxed, with smaller but growing communities of local LGBTQ+ and expats.

Cultural Insights

Argentinians value socializing, food (especially wine in Mendoza, as you'll find), family, and cultural life. Spanish is essential for deeper engagement; while English may be spoken in some tourist contexts, immersion helps. The pace tends to be lively and urban in BuenosAires, but more provincial elsewhere.

* * *

México – Puerto Vallarta (Jalisco)

Legal Protections

Located in Jalisco, Puerto Vallarta benefits from state-level protections prohibiting discrimination based on sexual orientation and gender identity. Same-sex marriage is legal and recognized.

Safety

Puerto Vallarta is one of the safest and most LGBTQ+ friendly destinations in México. It has an internationally recognized queer scene, particularly in the Zona Romántica. Caution is always wise, but the city is welcoming and well-patrolled.

Cost of Living

Costs can vary by area. Oceanfront and tourist-heavy neighborhoods are more expensive, while inland regions are more affordable. Generally, inland areas are more affordable than U.S. or European beach destinations.

Healthcare

Puerto Vallarta offers access to both public and private healthcare. Many clinics are accustomed to serving LGBTQ+ tourists and expats. Gender-affirming care may require travel to Guadalajara or México City.

Community

The city is a hub for LGBTQ+ tourism in Latin America. It has a strong queer infrastructure: resorts, bars, beach clubs, and an active Pride festival. The expat and digital nomad scene is also very inclusive.

Cultural Insights

Tourism shapes local culture—English is widely spoken in the hospitality sector. Socializing happens around beaches, bars, and cafés. The vibe is laid-back and community-driven.

* * *

México – México City (CDMX)

Legal Protections

CDMX is a national leader in LGBTQ+ rights, having legalized same-sex marriage and adoption early on. Anti-discrimination laws protect gender identity and sexual orientation.

Safety

Zona Rosa is the center of LGBTQ+ life and is generally safe. Common-sense precautions should be taken, like in any major city, especially at night. LGBTQ-targeted violence is rare in central areas.

Cost of Living

Varies greatly by neighborhood. Trendy areas like Roma, Condesa, and Polanco are more expensive. However, CDMX remains affordable compared to cities like New York or London.

Healthcare

Offers some of the best healthcare options in Latin America, both public and private. LGBTQ+ health services, including hormone therapy and HIV prevention/treatment, are widely available.

Community

The city has a large, diverse queer community with numerous organizations, events, and nightlife options. It hosts one of the largest Pride parades in Latin America.

Cultural Insights

Fast-paced, cosmopolitan, and progressive. English is spoken in tourist zones, but Spanish is essential for deeper integration. The arts, food, and cultural scenes are prosperous and inclusive.

* * *

México – Guadalajara (Jalisco)

Legal Protections

As the capital of Jalisco, Guadalajara is under state laws that legalize same-sex marriage and protect against discrimination based on gender identity and sexual orientation.

Safety

Generally safe in central and LGBTQ+ friendly neighborhoods. The city has a visible queer scene and is considered the "gay capital" of México after CDMX and Puerto Vallarta.

Cost of Living

More affordable than México City and beach destinations. Offers good value for housing, food, and entertainment.

Healthcare

Solid healthcare infrastructure. Public and private providers exist, though travel to CDMX may be required for specialized care (e.g., gender-affirming procedures).

Community

It has a vibrant LGBTQ+ scene with bars, clubs (like Envy and Babel), and annual events such as Guadalajara Pride. The arts and student communities contribute to its open-mindedness.

Cultural Insights

Deeply rooted in Mexican tradition but also modern and creative. Spanish is essential, but tourists and younger circles speak some English, and it is known for mariachi, tequila, and culture.

* * *

México – Playa del Carmen & Tulum (Riviera Maya)

Legal Protections

It is located in Quintana Roo, which recognizes same-sex marriage and has anti-discrimination laws. Legal protections are on par with those of other progressive Mexican states.

Safety

Popular tourist areas like Playa and Tulum are very LGBTQ+ friendly, though caution is still advised, especially at night or in isolated areas.

Cost of Living

Due to tourism and international demand, these are among the more expensive destinations in México. Rents and dining in central or beachfront areas are high.

Healthcare

Basic healthcare is widely available, and some clinics cater to expats and tourists. For advanced or LGBTQ+-specific care, travel to Cancun or México City may be needed.

Community

Both cities have growing queer communities, especially among expats and digital nomads. LGBTQ+ spaces include bars like Club 69 in Playa and Red Room in Tulum.

Cultural Insights

Vibe is relaxed, spiritual, and health-conscious. Tulum especially draws yoga and wellness-oriented communities. Spanish helps local interactions, but English is widely spoken in tourist areas.

* * *

Best for Afro-Diaspora Connection

Ghana: Return to the Motherland

Cultural Insight for Black Women:

- No racial "othering", but expats may still feel class divides.
- Natural hair and dark skin are celebrated; beauty standards favor local features.
- Black Americans often feel a spiritual return, but be prepared for cultural differences in gender roles.
- You're seen as African, but foreign, which brings both privilege and responsibility.

* * *

Senegal

- **Cultural Relevance:** It has a deep African heritage and is known for music, art, and history tied to the African diaspora.
- **Language:** French is the official language, and Wolof is widely spoken.
- **Black Expat Presence:** Strong, including African Americans connecting with ancestral roots.
- **Cost of Living:** ~$800 – $1,200/month.

* * *

Rwanda

- **Cultural Relevance:** Known for stability, reconciliation efforts, and a strong African identity.
- **Language:** Kinyarwanda is the national language, and English and French are also official.
- **Black Expat Presence:** Growing, especially among entrepreneurs and returnees from the diaspora.
- **Cost of Living:** ~$800–$1,200/month.

* * *

Salvador, Brazil

Safety: Salvador is vibrant but has higher crime rates than some Latin American cities. Petty theft and pickpocketing are common in crowded markets and tourist zones. Most expats feel safe in middle-class and expat neighborhoods, especially when using trusted transportation and staying alert at night. **Cost of Living:** $1,500–$2,000/month is typical for a single person. A one-bedroom apartment in a good neighborhood runs $500–800/month. Fresh produce, seafood, and local dining are affordable, but imported goods are expensive. Domestic help is common and cheap for middle-class expats. **Cultural Welcome:** Salvador is considered the Afro-Brazilian capital. Over 80% of the population identifies as Black or mixed race, and the city pulses with African traditions in food, music, dance, and spirituality (Candomblé). Foreigners, especially African Americans, often feel a strong cultural connection here. Portuguese is essential, though many locals are patient with learners. **Healthcare:** Private healthcare is preferred by most expats. Brazil offers excellent specialists and hospitals in larger cities. Monthly private insurance ranges from $80–$200, depending on age and coverage. Public healthcare is free but often overcrowded. **Community:** Salvador has one of the richest Afro-diasporic cultures in the world. Expat

93

networks exist but are smaller than in São Paulo or Rio. Black women often feel an immediate sense of belonging because of the city's visible Black culture and heritage. Festivals, music schools, and dance collectives provide natural entry points for building friendships. **Why It Fits:** Salvador offers cultural familiarity for Black women, affordable living, access to beaches, and a deeply rooted Black community unlike elsewhere in the Americas. It's also a hub for music, art, and spiritual practice, making it an enriching place to retire or build a slower life abroad.

Cultural Insight for Black Women:

- Many Black women expats describe Salvador as liberating.
- Your hair, skin, and style are celebrated here rather than questioned. Local women may even see you as kin, making connecting easier.
- While colorism exists in Brazil, the sheer visibility of Blackness in Salvador means you're less likely to feel "othered" than in many other destinations.
- Still, learning Portuguese is the most significant factor in building deeper relationships and avoiding isolation.

* * *

South Africa: Vibrant Diversity and Dramatic Landscapes

Safety: Crime can be high; choose suburbs in Cape Town (Camps Bay, Sea Point) or Johannesburg (Parkhurst, Bryanston). **Cost of Living:** $1,200–$2,000/month outside tourist hotspots. **Cultural Welcome:** English is an official language; affluent Black, Coloured, Indian, and LGBTQ+ communities. **Healthcare:** World-class private hospitals; private insurance is affordable by global standards. **Community:** Dynamic arts, music, and culinary scenes; strong expat and local collaboration. **Why It Fits:** Unique blend of urban energy and wild beauty, multiple visa options, and a chance to engage with post-apartheid social progress.

Cultural Insight for Black Women:

- You are the majority in South Africa, no racial "code-switching" needed.
- There are class and ethnic divides, but race-based profiling is far less common.
- Beauty standards embrace melanin and natural hair.
- Some Americans experience reverse culture shock due to social expectations and politics.

Quick Snapshots: Safety & Support at a Glance

Country	Safety Rating	Maternal Health	LGBTQ+ Rights	Black Expat Vibe
Portugal	High	Excellent	Strong	Thriving scene
Mexico	Medium	Moderate	Moderate	Growing
Ghana	Medium	Moderate	Limited	Strong ancestral tie
South Africa	Low/Medium	Advanced (in cities)	Strong (legal), variable socially	High diaspora
Costa Rica	High	Strong	Strong	Peaceful, smaller
Panama	Medium	Moderate	Moderate	Accessible
Dominician Rep.	Medium	Moderate	Low	Afro-dominant
Brazil	Low/Medium	Decent in urban centers	Strong on Paper	Strong in Salvador
Columbia	Medium	Moderate	Moderate	Vibrant in Cartagena

These ratings blend statistical sources with lived experience. Black expats often report feeling safer from racial profiling and police harm abroad, even if other risks (petty theft, infrastructure) exist.

City vs. City: Same Country, Different Vibe

Country	City 1	City 2	What to Know
Portugal	Lisbon	Porto	Lisbon is cosmopolitan, faster-paced; Porto is smaller, more local charm.
Ghana	Accra	Kumasi	Accra is modern, expensive, and international; Kumasi is more traditional and spiritual.
Mexico	Mérida	Mexico City	Mérida is safe, quiet, very local; CDMX is big, artistic, fast-moving.
Panama	Panama City	Boquete	Panama City is urban and modern; Boquete is calm, cool, and popular with retirees.
Brazil	Salvador	São Paulo	Salvador is the Black cultural capital; São Paulo is Brazil's NYC—busy, diverse, intense.
Costa Rica	San José	Tamarindo	San José has everything a capital offers; Tamarindo is slower, beachy, expat-heavy.

***Always research the city, not just the country. Culture, cost, and connection can vary drastically.

Honorable Mentions

- Ecuador (Cuenca): Eternal spring climate, small expat town, cheap healthcare.
- Thailand (Chiang Mai): Spiritual undercurrents, low cost of living, extensive expat infrastructure.
- Vietnam (Da Nang, Hoi An): Rapidly developing, affordable, and blending old and new.
- Georgia (Tbilisi): Visa-free entry for many, emerging digital nomad hub, low taxes.

Afro-Latino / African Diaspora Hotspots

For many Black women, connection to ancestral roots, artistic expression, and community care are non-negotiables. These three cities stand out for their rich African influence and welcoming Black energy.

* * *

Cartagena, Colombia

- **Cultural Relevance:** Caribbean soul with deep Afro-Colombian Pride, visible in music, food, and festivals.
- **Language:** Spanish required to engage meaningfully.
- **Black Expat Presence:** Small but passionate; many report feeling seen.
- **Cost of Living:** ~$700–$1,100/month

* * *

Santo Domingo, DR

- **Cultural Relevance:** One of the most Afro-identified countries in the Caribbean. List item #1
- **Language:** Spanish is essential.
- **Black Expat Presence:** Growing, especially among returning diaspora.
- **Cost of Living:** ~$650–$1,000/month

* * *

Puerto Vallarta

- **Cultural Relevance:** Popular resort city in México with increasing interest from Afro-Latinx and Black expats.
- **Language:** Spanish is helpful for integration, though English is the everyday language in tourist zones.
- **Black Expat Presence:** Small but visible, often connected through social groups and cultural events.
- **Cost of Living:** ~$900–$1,400/month.

* * *

Bali

- **Cultural Relevance: An** Indonesian island with a vibrant arts scene and
- International community.
- **Language:** Bahasa Indonesia is useful, but English is widely spoken in expat areas.
- **Black Expat Presence:** Active, mainly digital nomads and creatives in Canggu and Ubud.
- **Cost of Living:** ~$700–$1,200/month.

* * *

Veracruz

- **Cultural Relevance:** Historic port city in México with deep Afro-Mexican roots and vibrant music and dance traditions.
- **Language:** Spanish is essential.
- **Black Expat Presence:** Small, mainly cultural enthusiasts and researchers.
- **Cost of Living:** ~$700–$1,200/month.

* * *

Jamaica

- **Cultural Relevance:** One of the most Afro-identified countries in the
- Caribbean.
- **Language:** English is the official language, and Jamaican Patois is widely spoken.
- **Black Expat Presence:** Strong, including returning diaspora and entrepreneurs.
- **Cost of Living:** ~$750–$1,200/month.

* * *

The Gambia

- **Cultural Relevance:** Known for hospitality, traditional culture, and historic ties to the transatlantic slave trade.
- **Language:** English is the official language; local languages include Mandinka and Wolof.
- **Black Expat Presence:** Growing, with many diaspora returnees.
- **Cost of Living:** ~$600–$1,000/month.

* * *

Tulum

- **Relevance:** Beach town with strong eco-tourism, Mayan history, and wellness culture.
- **Language:** Spanish is essential; English is used daily in everyday areas.
- **Black Expat Presence:** Small but visible, mostly digital nomads and creative professionals.
- **Cost of Living:** ~$1,000–$1,800/month.

* * *

Kenya

- **Cultural Relevance:** Rich mix of African traditions and modern urban culture, with strong diasporic ties.
- **Language:** English and Swahili are official.
- **Black Expat Presence:** Strong, especially in Nairobi and Mombasa.
- **Cost of Living:** ~$900–$1,400/month.

* * *

Merida

- **Cultural Relevance:** Popular tourist destination in México's Riviera Maya with a growing expat community.
- **Language:** Spanish is essential; English is widely spoken in tourist areas.
- **Black Expat Presence:** Small but growing, connected through digital nomad and travel communities.
- **Cost of Living:** ~$900–$1,500/month.

Firsthand Perspective:

I was nervous about moving to México, but once I started taking Spanish classes and making local friends, I realized how affordable and welcoming life here can be."

– **Black eMéridaMérida**

* * *

Peru

- **Cultural Relevance:** Strong Indigenous, Afro-Peruvian, and Spanish heritage, especially vibrant in coastal cities like Lima.
- **Language:** Spanish is essential; some Quechua is spoken in the Andes.
- **Black Expat Presence:** Small but growing, centered in Lima and Cusco, with community ties to Afro-Peruvian culture.
- **Cost of Living:** ~$800–$1,300/month.

* * *

México City

- **Cultural Relevance:** Capital city with diverse culture, history, and a growing Afro-Mexican awareness.
- **Language:** Spanish is essential; English is standard in business and tourist areas.
- **Black Expat Presence:** Moderate, including entrepreneurs, remote workers, and cultural enthusiasts
- **Cost of Living:** ~$1,000–$1,800/month.

* * *

Burkina Faso

- **Cultural Relevance:** Known for stability, reconciliation efforts, and a strong African identity.
- **Language:** Kinyarwanda is the national language; English and French are also
- Official.
- **Black Expat Presence:** Growing, especially among entrepreneurs and returnees from the diaspora.
- **Cost of Living:** ~$800–$1,200/month.

* * *

Play Del Carmen

- **Cultural Relevance:** Popular tourist destination in México's Riviera Maya with a growing expat community.
- **Language:** Spanish is essential; English is widely spoken in tourist areas.
- **Black Expat Presence:** Small but growing, connected through digital nomad and travel communities.
- **Cost of Living:** ~$900–$1,500/month.

* * *

Guadalajara

- **Cultural Relevance:** Major cultural hub in western México, known for mariachi, tequila, and colonial architecture.
- **Language:** Spanish is essential; English is spoken in some business and tourist areas.
- **Black Expat Presence:** Small but growing, mainly digital nomads and creative professionals.
- **Cost of Living:** ~$900–$1,500/month.

Reflection Prompts:

- Which country feels most like a mirror of my dreams?
- What are my non-negotiables (language, climate, proximity to home)?

· What questions do I need to research for my top three picks?

Affirmation:

"My spirit will recognize where I am meant to land."

"I don't need to know everything to take the first step."

Choosing where to go is as personal as deciding whom to love. Let your intuition guide you, then back it up with research.

Chapter 5: Creating a Soft Life Abroad (Without Apology)

You didn't leave the grind to recreate it overseas.

This chapter is about designing a life that feels gentle, abundant, and liberating, a "soft life" that honors your worth.

What the "Soft Life" Really Means

A soft life is not about extravagance or indulgence for its own sake. It's about choosing ease over hustle, presence over productivity, and self-respect over self-sacrifice. It's a radical act of self-care and self-recognition.

Elements of the soft life:

- Intentional Slowness: Embracing a pace that allows room for breathing, reflection, and spontaneity.
- Sensory Delight: Surrounding yourself with colors, textures, tastes,
- And sounds that uplift you.
- Boundaried Time: Protecting your hours for Rest, creativity, and relationships, without guilt.
- Purposeful Indulgence: Allocating resources to what genuinely brings you joy (a weekly market visit, a local massage, a community class).

* * *

What Soft Life Looks Like

Soft Life in Portugal

- Long, slow lunches with friends without checking the clock.
- Affordable fresh seafood and produce from neighborhood markets.
- Walking along the coast after work with no rush-hour traffic.

Soft Life in Thailand

- Hiring a weekly housekeeper for less than a U.S. manicure.

- Getting $8 massages in open-air spas after grocery shopping.
- Renting a fully furnished apartment with pool access for under $500/month.

Soft Life in Ghana

- Living near extended family and reconnecting with traditions.
- Affordable tailor-made clothing in African prints.
- Attending cultural festivals where you are part of the majority.

Soft Life in Mexico

- Fresh flowers on your table every week for $5.
- Morning walks in safe, tree-lined neighborhoods.
- Daily fresh-pressed juice from the market for less than a U.S. coffee.

Designing Daily Rituals Rooted in Joy, Peace, and Pleasure

Rituals anchor us. They transform ordinary days into practices of fulfillment.

Morning Rite:

- Wake without an alarm clock (if possible) or set a gentle tone with soft lighting.
- Hydrate with warm water, tea, or juice from local fruits.
- Spend 10 minutes stretching, journaling, or meditating to align your mind and body.

Midday Pause:

- Take a walk to a nearby café, park, or market stall.
- Savor a meal at your own pace, mindful of flavors, colors, and textures.
- Include a creative practice: photography, sketching, or observing your

environment.

Evening Unwind:

- Create a tech curfew (no screens 1–2 hours before bed).
- Indulge in a bath, herbal tea, or a few chapters of a favorite book. Reflect on one moment of gratitude and one intention for tomorrow.

Financial Ease as a Freedom Strategy

Soft living isn't about spending willy-nilly; it's about aligning spending with what fuels your well-being.

Budget for Bliss:

- Identify the top three experiences that bring you joy (e.g., weekend beach trips, cooking classes, local artistry).
- Allocate a fixed portion of your monthly budget to those experiences before anything else.

Automate Abundance:

- Use community networks for bartering services (e.g., language tutoring in exchange for yoga classes).
- Explore local crafts markets for unique decor or gifts at lower prices than tourist shops.

Hacks for Affordable Luxury:

- Use community networks for bartering services (e.g., language tutoring in exchange for yoga classes).
- Explore local crafts markets for unique decor or gifts at lower prices than tourist shops.

* * *

Releasing Guilt About Rest and Ease

Shifting your beliefs is key if you've been conditioned to associate Rest with laziness. As Black women, we've often been taught that Rest is a luxury we haven't earned. But Rest is not a reward, it's reparations. The softness you create abroad isn't a betrayal of your strength. It's a return to your wholeness.

Reframe Rest as Resistance:

- In systems that reward overwork, taking time for yourself is an act of defiance.
- Remind yourself: your value is intrinsic, not tied to output.

Challenge the "Hustle Heartbeat":

- When you catch yourself apologizing for downtime, pause and affirm: "I deserve this Rest."
- Journal about moments when Rest led to creativity, clarity, or improved relationships.

Building Community Rooted in Care, Not Comparison

Find Your Circle:

- Seek local groups that align with your interests, such as book clubs, expat meetups, art classes, and wellness circles.
- Prioritize in-person gatherings; digital groups can supplement, but face-to-face builds deeper bonds.

Practice Generosity:

- Offer your skills or support first. Teaching a friend to bake bread, hosting a small potluck, or sharing language tips fosters reciprocity.
- Celebrate others' successes without envy. Their joy doesn't diminish your own.

Cultivate Rituals Together:

- Establish a weekly brunch, a monthly excursion, or a shared creative project.
- These recurring touchpoints become the scaffolding of your social support.

Reflection Prompts:

- What rituals can I introduce tomorrow to honor my need for softness?
- Where am I still guilty about Rest, and how can I reframe it? Who can I invite into a mutual care circle, and what can I offer them?
- Designing a soft life abroad isn't passive. It's intentional, radical, and transformative. And you are fully deserving of every gentle moment you create.

Affirmation:
"Abundance is not tied to one country or one job."
"I am the source of my security... not my employer, not a paycheck."

Chapter 6: Navigating Culture Shock & Settling In

Even paradise has paperwork. Even beauty can feel disorienting.

This chapter is your emotional survival kit for settling in — a guide to embracing the unfamiliar with grace, respect, and a sense of adventure.

The Four Phases of Culture Shock

Stage	What It Feels Like	Coping Strategy
Honeymoon Phase	Everything feels new and exciting. You romanticize daily life.	Explore, take photos, enjoy the novelty. Keep notes of what you love for later. Start a Journal
Ffrustration Phase	Language barriers, bureaucracy, and cultural differences feel overwhelming	Learn key phrases, ask for help, focus on small wins. Name your feelings without judgement, and practice self compassion.
Adjustment Phase	You develop routines, understand local norms, and feel less like an outsider.	Build a support network, try new hobbies, and maintain contact with loved ones. Celebrate small wins, like ordering food in the local language, or making a new friend.
Acceptance Phase	You feel at home. Cultural differences no longer frustrate you.	Share your knowledge, mentor new arrivals, and continue learning. Reflect on your transformation and how far you've come.

My Personal Experience with Culture Shock and Community

Let me be straight with you: Culture shock isn't only about the new country it's about the possible expat circus you land in, too, and I'm going to walk you through how I lived every stage of it. Disclaimer: My Experience is not indicative of the normal experience. I am just giving you the possible worst-case scenario.

When I first moved abroad, I thought the expat community would be all love and support. I thought folks would look out for each other. Surprisingly, my culture shock didn't come from locals. It came from other expats showing their ass.

Stage 1: Honeymoon

At first, I was starry-eyed. Everything looked perfect—the food, the weather, the freedom. I thought, "This is it; I made it." I took all the pictures, journaled, and made self-care a daily practice. But once I started looking for real community, that honeymoon vibe disappeared quickly.

Stage 2: Frustration

This is when the mask came off.

Gatekeeping

Some of these mofos treated basic info like it was the damn nuclear codes. They only shared property buying, remote jobs, and visa hacks with their clique. And let's be clear, some didn't want fellow Black women or men to have access because they didn't want anyone possibly outshining them. That pissed me off. I wasn't about to beg some half-helpful ass expat to drop crumbs. So, I researched, connected with locals, joined open groups, and shared what I knew with people who weren't afraid of seeing others win.

Overpriced Events

Half the meetups I saw were "community" dinners at $200 restaurants. That ain't community, that's a hustle. Folks play dress-up to look essential and collect money. I tried that shit once, maybe twice. Then I said hell no. I started attending free events, volunteering, and having people over for a meal that didn't break the bank. Guess what? That's where I met real people.

No Local Integration

This one blew my mind. Some expats pack up their lives, move across the ocean, and then stay stuck in an American bubble. No language, no local friends, no respect for the culture they're living in. I thought, "Why did you even leave the States?" I wasn't about to do that. I learned greetings, spoke to my neighbors, and attended local festivals. That's how I built real friendships and felt like I belonged.

Drama-Heavy Spaces

Then came the gossip. Lord. Who's broke? Who's sleeping with whom? Who's "failing" at business? Who's lying about going back to the States? All this messy shit like we were still in high school. I listened, but I didn't join in.

I removed myself from the cliques and invested in relationships with people who wanted growth, not gossip.

Predatory Behavior and Classism

Some expats are predators, period. They size you up by your wallet, job, and address. If you don't look "luxury," you're dismissed. That stung at first, but then I realized, why the hell am I trying to prove myself to broke-spirited people flexing like they're rich? I stopped chasing approval. I put my energy into people who value respect and integrity.

Lack of Safety and Performative Allyship

The fakest thing I saw was groups yelling "diversity" while silencing Black voices. They wanted us in their photos, not in their leadership. They didn't protect people from harassment. They only engaged with you if they could profit. That's when I learned: not every space with "inclusion" stamped on it is safe. I set boundaries, left the bullshit behind, and found communities that honored who I was.

Stage 3: Adjustment

Once I stopped wasting time with fake-ass spaces, things shifted. I learned how to spot the red flags. I eventually found locals who treated me like family. I linked with expats who were about community, not competition. I had officially passed the adjustment phase.

Stage 4: Acceptance

Here's the hard truth: shady Western behavior doesn't disappear overseas. Some people bring the same toxic, greedy mindset with them. Once I accepted that, I stopped expecting everybody to act right. I don't need to be everywhere. I don't need to fit into every group. I need my people. The ones who share information within our community. The ones who respect boundaries. The ones who don't give a shit about status games. That's my tribe. And with them, life abroad is worth it.

Other than the expat community shenanigans, I would have to say the biggest shock for me wasn't the food, the language, or even the weather. It was realizing that almost everything I'd been fed about the world, and even the region I now live in, was bullshit. School, TV, the media, all lies. I was offended and appalled. Please don't take their word for it; do your own research. Connect with American Immigrants, currently residing in the region of your choice. Lastly, go check it out for yourself.

I grew up in NYC, in a super diverse community, so I'm naturally curious about culture. Nothing else really shocks me. And Jamaica? It's my favorite place on earth. From there, I learned to slow down, be patient, and stop rushing everything. Those lessons saved me more than once.

Look, my story is the worst-case scenario. Not everyone's culture shock will look like mine. But knowing what's possible keeps you from getting blindsided. The shock is real, but being prepared makes it manageable.

Creating Routines That Ground You

Routines are stabilizers when everything else feels changeable.

- Morning Grounding: breathing exercises.
- Weekly Rituals: Start with something consistent, a cup of tea, a short walk, or a few minutes of exercise. Choose one or two days for special activities, farmers' markets, language exchange meetups, or nature hikes.
- Work–life Boundaries: Define your workspace (even if it's a corner of your room) and set clear on/off times if you work remotely.

Consistency nurtures a sense of safety and control, even in a new context.

Learning the Language (Even If Just the Basics)

Language is the gateway to community.

- Essential Phrases: Learn greetings, thank-yous, numbers, and directions first.
- Daily Practice: First, learn greetings, thank-yous, numbers, and directions. Label items in your home, use flashcard apps for 10 minutes daily, or practice with a language partner.
- Immersion: Listen to local radio, watch local TV shows with subtitles, or tune into neighborhood conversations.

Even a small vocabulary builds confidence and opens doors to deeper cultural understanding.

Discovering Your Local Favorites

Find your own map of comfort and delight:

- Favorite Café: A place where the staff know your name and your order.
- Walking Route: A safe, scenic loop that energizes you.
- Market Vendor: The person always has the ripest fruit or the freshest bread.

These anchors turn a foreign place into a familiar neighborhood.

Making Friends and Holding Space for Homesickness

Building Genuine Connections:

- Join interest-based groups (art classes, sports, volunteer projects).

- Attend expat meetups as well as local gatherings to balance perspectives.
- Host small get-togethers, potlucks, or group outings.

Embracing Homesickness:

- Acknowledge that missing home is natural and temporary.
- Create a "comfort corner" with photos, familiar snacks, or items that remind you of loved ones.
- Schedule regular calls with friends and family, but limit them to avoid isolation in your new locale.

Finding Your People Abroad (and Not Just Any People)

When you land in a new country, you need two things ASAP:

1. An income stream you can manage from anywhere (if you're working).
2. An income stream you can manage from anywhere (if you're working).

Here's how to make both happen without wasting months in cliquey, unhelpful spaces.

Remote Work Hubs with a Strong Black Presence

Because not all coworking spaces feel like home.

- AfriBlocks: Global African & diaspora freelancer network.
- Black Remote She: Safe space for Black women remote workers.
- Outpost: Coworking + coliving with built-in community (Bali, Cambodia, more).
- Nomadness Travel Tribe: Black travelers & nomads worldwide

- Therapy for Black Girls – International List: For mental health support abroad.

Building Your Chosen Family Abroad

Let's be real — the expat "scene" can be full of folks who want to gossip, gatekeep, or show off. Your chosen family? That's different. These are the people who make your new country feel like yours. Tips:

- Seek out shared values, not just shared passports.
- Say yes to small invites, dinner at someone's home is worth more than ten "expat happy hours."
- Show up for others before you need them.

Forming Peer Groups that Actually Work

If you can't find a group you like, create one:

- Theme it (Sunday potluck, hiking crew, book club, skill-share).
- Keep it consistent (same day/time).
- Mix locals and expats to avoid living in a bubble.

Building Your Support System Abroad (Without the Drama)

When you move abroad, the people you choose to let into your circle matter as much as where you live. The wrong group can drain your spirit; the right one can feel like home. Here's how to make sure you choose wisely.

1. Vetting an Expat Group Before You Join

Fill this out before committing time, energy, or membership fees.

Question	Notes
Who runs the group and why did they start it?	
Does the mission align with my values (unity, support, cultural respect)?	
Are members welcoming to newcomers?	
Is it inclusive of different backgrounds and identities?	
What kind of events do they host (family-friendly, professional, cultural)?	
Do they support integration with the local community?	
Is there a mix of locals and expats, or is it a closed bubble?	
How is conflict handled?	
Are meetups affordable and accessible?	
How will joining this group improve my life abroad?	

2. Community Checklist

Use this to decide whether a group or community space is worth your time:

☐ Welcomes diversity (age, nationality, identity)

☐ Encourages cultural exchange with locals

☐ Offers practical support for newcomers (housing tips, visa help, job leads)

☐ Creates safe spaces for open conversation

☐ Regularly hosts in-person gatherings Affordable to participate in

☐ Has a clear code of conduct or group rules

☐ Members speak respectfully online and offline

☐ Promotes unity over competition

3. Red Flags to Avoid in Expat Network

If you spot more than one of these, keep walking, Loved One:

- **Gatekeeping** – They decide who's "worthy" of information.
- **Overpriced Events** – If every meetup is at a $200 restaurant, it's not about community.
- **No Local Integration** – Only hanging out in expat bubbles, ignoring the host culture.
- **Drama-Heavy** – Gossip, cliques, and constant arguments.
- **Predatory Behavior** – Financial, emotional, or romantic exploitation of newcomers.
- **Classism** – Ranking people by income, job title, or where they live.

- **Lack of Safety** – No protocols for harassment or inappropriate conduct.
- **Performative Allyship** – Intercultural Groups Claiming inclusivity but ignoring or silencing Black voices.

Tip: A group can look perfect on social media but be a hot mess in real life. Trust your gut; if the energy feels off or does not align with your moral compass, you don't owe them your time.

Being a Good Visitor and Respectful Neighbor

Observe and Adapt:

- Learn local norms around greetings, dress codes, and social etiquette.
- Respect public spaces — keep noise levels appropriate and dispose of waste responsibly.

Contribute Positively:

- Support local businesses by shopping, dining, and using services.
- Volunteer with community projects or donate skills pro bono (teaching English, offering professional expertise).

Avoid Cultural Imperialism:

- Listen more than you speak; ask questions instead of assuming.
- Refrain from criticizing customs or imposing your own values.
- Embrace differences as opportunities for growth, not problems to fix.

Navigating culture shock and integrating respectfully isn't just about survival; it's about thriving as a global citizen who brings curiosity, humility, and care wherever you go.

Affirmation:

I receive each new sight, sound, and flavor with joy and curiosity.

I give myself grace when things feel hard. I am learning, and that is enough.

I celebrate small wins and honor how far I've come in creating my new life.

I am rooted here. I carry the best of where I came from and embrace where I am now.

Chapter 7: Raising Children Abroad (Family Freedom)

Your kids deserve peace, too. Moving as a family is both an incredible adventure and a profound responsibility. This chapter equips you with the tools to raise confident, joyful, and globally minded children, without forfeiting their sense of security or cultural identity.

Living It: Parent Perspectives:

Yolanda, U.S. to Belize, mother of 1 (age 6) "Our daughter's school day is shorter, which gives us more family time. The downside is fewer extracurriculars, so we create our own, beach cleanups, art projects, and cooking together."

Educational Options: Finding the Right Fit

I don't have school-age children myself, but I've been a kind of "bonus" or co-grandparent for a friend and neighbor whose grandchild has been living abroad since he was just four weeks old. School works differently abroad. Daycare is more affordable, and children in my area often start school earlier than in the U.S. Her grandson is only three. Yet, he already wears a school uniform, carries books, and follows a structured daily routine. When his mother had to return to work in the United States, she chose to leave him with family. Her decision wasn't just about logistics; she saw the benefit of his becoming bilingual from such a young age. She now pays him about $300 monthly to attend a private school. I'm sure tuition will increase as he ages, but it's nowhere near the $2,400+ a month she'd be paying for daycare back in America.

Local Public Schools

- Culturally immersive and often free or low-cost.
- Language immersion accelerates bilingualism but may require support for transitions.
- Check for international programs or bilingual tracks.
- **Enrollment checklist:** passport, child's birth certificate, proof of residence, vaccination records, and previous school transcripts.

International Schools

- Follow American, British, IB, or other curricula in English.
- Higher tuition costs but smoother academic continuity for return visas or eventual repatriation.
- Strong expat community and extracurricular offerings.
- **Enrollment checklist:** same as above, plus admission exams and application fees.

Private and Alternative Schools

- Montessori, Waldorf, or other progressive models focusing on holistic development.
- Often, smaller class sizes and project-based learning are used.
- Tuition varies widely; research scholarships or sliding-scale options are available.

Homeschooling / Unschooling

- Complete control over curriculum and schedule.
- Blends travel experiences, local culture, and individualized study.
- Requires dedication, a support network, and compliance with U.S. and local laws.

Tip: Visit schools in person if possible. Talk to other expat parents about their children's experiences.

Cost Comparison: Childcare in the U.S. vs Abroad

Type of Care	United States (Average Monthly Cost)	Abroad (Example: Private School/Daycare in Latin America)
Infant/Toddler Daycare (Full-Time)	$2,400+	$250–$350
Preschool (3–5 years)	$1,000–$1,500	$200–$400
After-School Care	$500–$800	$50–$150
Nanny (Full-Time)	$3,000–$4,500	$400–$800
Private School (Primary Grades)	$1,500–$2,500	$300–$600

Why It's Cheaper Abroad

- Lower cost of living means tuition and salaries are significantly less.
- Uniforms & supplies are often required but still cost less than U.S. fees.
- Early start ages mean kids enter structured programs sooner, often at lower rates than American daycare.
- Many programs include meals, transportation, or extracurriculars in the monthly fee.

Tip: If you're moving with kids, research local and international school costs before relocating. In many countries, you can get a safe, high-quality education for your child for a fraction of what you'd pay in the States, without sacrificing academics or care.

Questions to Ask International Schools

- What curriculum do you follow?
- How diverse are your students and staff? Which languages are taught?
- What safety policies are in place?
- How do you support children new to the country?
- Helping Kids Cope with Culture Shock
- Children move through the four phases of culture shock differently from

adults.

* * *

Helping Kids Cope with Culture Shock

Children move through the four phases of culture shock differently from adults.

Living It: Parent Perspectives:
  Danielle, U.S. to Thailand, single mom of 3 (ages 5, 8, 14) "Private international schools here cost a fraction of what we'd pay in the States. The kids are learning Thai and making friends from all over the world."

1. **Honeymoon Phase:** Everything feels exciting and new. Take advantage of curiosity with local adventures.
2. **Frustration Phase:** Homesickness, language struggles, or missing old friends may appear. Keep routines consistent and validate feelings.
3. **Adjustment Phase:** Kids begin to adapt, making friends, enjoying foods, and using local phrases. Encourage independence in small tasks.
4. **Adaptation Phase:** Make the new country feel like home. Keep cultural connections to the U.S. alive while celebrating local traditions.

Emotional Transitions and Identity Development
  One of the most profound shifts mothers report is seeing their Black children treated as children. Abroad, they're less likely to be seen as threats, suspended for expressing emotion, or funneled into trauma. This doesn't erase racism but opens space for joy, curiosity, and full-bodied growth.

Children experience cultural transitions differently by age:

Young Children (3–7): and traditions. Adapt quickly to new routines and languages, but may miss familiar faces. Social Integration Tips: Enroll in local art, dance, or swim classes. Use bilingual picture books—host small playdates with neighbors.

Tweens (8–12): Desire both freedom and familiarity. Peer relationships matter deeply. Social Integration Tips: Encourage extracurriculars, sports, music, and coding clubs. Use online video calls to maintain U.S. friendships.

Teens (13+): Value autonomy and peer identity. They may resist change; involve them in planning and decision-making. Social Integration Tips: Give them input in activities and peer groups. Encourage volunteering or internships for local integration.

Living It: Parent Perspectives:

  Marcus, U.S. to Ghana, father of 1 (age 12) "We wanted our son to grow up where he's not the only Black kid in class. In Accra, he's thriving, but we've had to adjust to differences in teaching style, more emphasis on rote learning."

Strategies for Emotional Support:

- Maintain open conversations about feelings; validate homesickness as usual.
- Encourage creative expression: drawing, storytelling, or journaling about their experiences.
- Create rituals that honor their heritage: cooking family recipes, celebrating U.S. holidays.

Custody, Co-Parenting, and Legal Logistics

If you share custody or co-parent from afar, precise legal planning is essential:

- **Court Orders:** Update custody agreements to specify international travel permissions.
- Power of Attorney: Grant trusted individuals authority for school decisions or emergencies.
- **Medical Consent Letter:** Required for emergencies abroad (include translations if possible).
- **Single Parent Travel:** Some countries require notarized consent from
- The non-traveling parent.
- **Dual Residency Planning:** Determine both countries' school obligations, tax implications, and healthcare coverage.
- **Emergency Plans:** Identify nearby contacts, pediatricians, and clinics;
- Prepare a medical consent letter.

International Travel with Children Checklist

- Passport (valid for at least 6 months)
- Notarized consent letter if traveling without the other parent, Copies of custody agreements
- Child's vaccination record
- Emergency contacts in both countries

Pro Tip: Consult an international family law attorney to ensure all jurisdictions recognize your documents.

Building Community as a Family

A strong support network is key for both parents and children:

- **Expat Parent Groups:** Facebook, WhatsApp, and Meetup often have localized family communities.
- **Playdates and Learning Pods:** Organize or join informal learning pods or social gatherings. Great for homeschool families.
- **Enroll in local cultural clubs.** Museum programs, sports teams, and music or dance classes can foster friendships with local kids.
- **Library and Language Centers:** Many host story hours, language classes, and cultural events for families.
- **Family Volunteer Opportunities:** Soup kitchens, beach cleanups, animal shelters, and building community roots.

Safety Abroad for Children

Teach Your Kids:

- Their full name, address, and phone number in the new country.

- How to say basic emergency phrases in the local language.
- Who are safe adults (police, teachers, neighbors)?

Post Local Emergency Numbers: Keep them by the phone and in your child's backpack.

Living It: Parent Perspectives:

Angela, U.S. to Portugal, mother of 2 (ages 7 and 10) "The biggest surprise was how safe I felt letting my kids walk to the bakery. In Lisbon, it's normal for children to have independence, and the community looks out for them."

* * *

Family Routine Transition Plan (First 90 Days)

Week 1–4:

- Keep morning/bedtime routines familiar.
- Explore local grocery stores and parks.

Week 5–8:

- Introduce one local tradition each week (food, music, holiday).
- Schedule regular check-ins with kids to talk about feelings.

Week 9–12:

- Enroll in one regular extracurricular.
- Start hosting or attending social events with other families.

Creating a Childhood Your Kids Don't Have to Recover From

Your children should leave this experience with pride, not confusion.

- **Balance:** Keep favorite toys, stories, and family traditions while embracing local culture.
- **Empowerment:** Teach them to navigate simple tasks: ordering food,
- Asking for directions, using public transit.
- **Reflection:** Use photo albums or travel journals to document milestones and memories.
- **Gratitude Practices:** Reflection Prompts: Weekly "3 things I love here" to encourage positive focus.

* * *

Reflection Prompts:

- How can I involve my children in decisions about schools and routines?
- What traditions from home do we want to preserve, and what new ones would we like to create?
- Which local activities can help my child build confidence and friendships?

Raising children abroad is both a gift and a journey of mutual growth. With planning and emotional attunement, you can craft a family life as rich in belonging as adventure.

Affirmation:

"My children deserve to see me safe, soft, and whole."
    "Breaking cycles starts with me, even if it looks unfamiliar."

Chapter 8: Retiring Abroad (Freedom Isn't Just for the Young)

Your golden years should be golden. Not gray, not stressful, not lonely.

Retirement abroad isn't just a way to stretch dollars; it's an opportunity to reclaim time, health, and purpose. It's the chance to swap "barely getting by" for "fully living," and to give your later years the richness and peace you've earned.

Sample Monthly Budgets for Retirees

Country & City	Rent (2BR)	Utilities + Internet	Groceries	Healthcare	LastLeisure/Tr avel Name	Totaal Monthly
Portugal- Algarve	$900	$150	$250	Mark$80 (public + private mix)	$200	$1,580
costa Rica - Atenas	$800	$120	$200	$100 (Caja + private visits)	$200	$1,420
Mexico - Merida	$650	$100	$180	$80 (private insurance)	$150	$1,160
Belize - Cayo District	$700	$100	$220	$120 (private)	$150	$1,290

Tip: Include a short note under the table reminding retirees to factor in flights home, currency exchange rates, and inflation.

Best Countries for Retirees on Fixed Incomes

Portugal

- **Visa:** D7 Passive Income Visa for retirees with €8,460 annual income requirement
- **Cost of Living:** $1,200–$2,000/month for comfortable coastal living in cities like Faro or Lisbon suburbs
- **Healthcare:** Public National Health Service (NHS) plus affordable private options
- **Community:** Active retiree enclaves in the Algarve; English is widely spoken

Mexico

- **Visa:** Temporary Resident Visa requires $2,500/month proof of income or $43,000 in savings

- **Cost of Living:** $1,000–$1,500/month in towns like Lake Chapala or Mérida
- **Healthcare:** Private insurance starting at $40/month; world-class private hospitals
- **Community:** Large American retiree communities with bilingual services

Costa Rica

- **Visa:** Pensionado Program requires $1,000/month pension income
- **Cost of Living:** $1,500–$2,000/month, including rent and healthcare
- **Healthcare:** Public (Caja) coverage for residents; supplemental private insurance available
- **Community:** Retiree networks in Atenas, Escazu, and coastal towns

Panama

- **Visa:** Pensionado Visa requires $1,000/month pension, includes discounts on utilities, travel, and entertainment
- **Cost of Living:** $1,500–$2,200/month; rental apartments in Boquete cost $600–$800/month
- **Healthcare:** High-quality private hospitals; public system accessible
- for residents
- **Community:** Pensionado discounts attract retirees nationwide; English is used in expat hubs

Ecuador (Cuenca)

- **Visa:** Pensioner Visa requires $800/month pension income
- **Cost of Living:** $800–$1,200/month for rent, groceries, and utilities
- **Healthcare:** Preventive care clinics at $20–$30/visit; private insurance is affordable
- **Community:** Small but active expat groups; historic city center with walkable amenities

Social Security Abroad

U.S. Social Security payments can be deposited into foreign bank accounts in many countries. Steps to set up:

- Enroll in direct deposit with SSA before you leave.
- Maintain a U.S. bank account on an international transfer service (Wise, OFX)
- Notify SSA of your foreign address and any required forms (SSA-1199)

Note: Some countries impose local taxes on foreign pensions; research treaties to avoid double taxation.

Affordable Healthcare and Housing

Aging in the U.S. is becoming more complicated and more expensive than ever.

In July 2025, the One Big Beautiful Bill Act cut nearly $900 billion—$1 trillion from Medicaid over the next decade. These cuts add work requirements, tighten eligibility, and could leave 11.8 million Americans without coverage. Rural hospitals and nursing homes are especially vulnerable, with 27% saying they'd have to close and 55% planning to limit admissions for Medicaid-dependent seniors.

This means fewer facilities, reduced staffing, higher out-of-pocket costs, and limited home-care services, all while Medicare benefits remain under political and budgetary pressure. For many U.S. seniors, "aging in place" may soon mean aging with less care and more financial strain.

Retiring abroad can offer:

- Lower-cost, quality healthcare (including geriatric and preventive care).
- Affordable housing without crushing property taxes. Safer, slower lifestyles with vibrant retiree communities.
- The ability to stretch Social Security or pension income into a truly comfortable life.

In today's climate, moving abroad is no longer just a dream... **It's a strategic retirement plan.**

Healthcare Tips:

- Enroll in local public plans when eligible; many countries offer resident rates.
- Purchase international expat health insurance for supplemental coverage.
- Consider medical tourism for elective procedures (dental, vision, cosmetic).
- Research geriatric care availability, in-home nursing, and aging support services.

Housing Strategies:

- Rent for 6–12 months before buying to test neighborhoods.
- Leverage pensionado or retiree discounts on utilities and property taxes.
- Work with local real estate agents specialized in retiree relocations

Geriatric Healthcare & Aging Support Abroad

Many countries offer high-quality, low-cost care for seniors, including:

- Preventive screenings and wellness programs. Affordable in-home assistance for daily living.
- Physical therapy and rehabilitation at a fraction of U.S. prices.

- Anti-aging treatments and wellness retreats are integrated into routine healthcare.

Social Integration for Seniors

- Clubs & Associations: Join local hobby groups, language exchanges, or expat meetups.
- Volunteering: Mentor youth, support animal shelters, or join environmental projects.
- Faith Communities: Many churches, mosques, and temples welcome expats warmly.
- Hobbies: Gardening, art classes, dance lessons, or hiking groups

My Perspective on Retiring Abroad

I see seniors overseas living the golden years that many in the U.S. only dream about. They can access affordable geriatric healthcare, anti-aging resources, and healthier foods. Their pensions or Social Security go further, giving them financial breathing room instead of forcing them back to work in their seventies. Many belong to vibrant social clubs, volunteer programs, and hobby groups that keep them mentally and socially active.

The grandparents I meet are especially inspiring; they often host their grandchildren for summer vacations abroad, giving them experiences many kids never get: extended time in another country, learning a new language, and making friends across cultures. I can't wait until my grandchildren are old enough so I can offer them the same gift. Children who travel internationally early in life grow more adaptable, curious, and culturally aware.

Benefits of Retiring Abroad vs. Staying in the U.S.

Retiring Abroad	Remaining in the U.S.
Lower cost of living, allowing pensions/Social Security to stretch further.	Rising living costs often outpace fixed incomes.
Affordable healthcare, including geriatric and preventive care.	Healthcare costs can be a major financial burden.
Access to fresh, healthy foods at lower prices.	Healthy food often more expensive than processed options.
Opportunities for bilingualism and cultural enrichment.	Limited cross-cultural experiences without travel.
Slower pace of life reduces stress and improves health.	Fast-paced lifestyle can contribute to stress and isolation.
Strong expat and local communities for social engagement.	Social isolation common among seniors, especially those living alone.
Ability to host family for extended, affordable visits.	Short visits often limited by high domestic travel and lodging costs.

Safety & Security Tips for Older Expats

- Keep emergency contacts both local and back home. Know the location of the nearest hospital or clinic.
- Use secure, reliable transportation options.
- Keep a valid will and power of attorney in your home and host country.
- Use online banking and fraud alerts to monitor accounts.

Reflection Prompts:

- What does a fulfilling retirement look like for me, beyond finances?
- Which community activities resonate with my passions?
- How can I balance exploration with routines that nurture my well-being?

Affirmation:

"I am not too old to start again, I am finally wise enough to begin."

"The life I want now doesn't need to match the one I've already lived."

"Rest is my reward. Joy is my right. Freedom is still mine to claim."

"My age is not a barrier; it proves I have survived enough to know what matters."

"I do not owe anyone more struggle...I have given enough."

Retirement abroad isn't an exile; it's an elevation of your life's next chapter. Your golden years are waiting; claim them.

Chapter 9: Love, Dating & Relationships Abroad

New country, new connections.

Romance and relationships abroad come with their own set of joys and challenges. This chapter guides you through building authentic, romantic, or platonic connections while honoring your liberation.

Dating Norms in Different Countries

Every culture has its own dance when it comes to dating:

- **Mediterranean (Portugal, Italy):** Slow, intentional courtship; meals can last hours.
- **Latin America (Mexico, Costa Rica):** Family-oriented; respect for elders and traditional gender roles.
- **West Africa (Ghana):** Community and family introductions; extended family approval can be critical.
- **Southeast Asia (Thailand):** Politeness and indirect communication; public displays of affection may be limited.
- **South Africa:** Diverse practices reflecting multiple cultures; open nightlife scenes in urban centers.

Research and observe local customs. When in doubt, ask graciously or follow local friends' lead.

* * *

Fetishization vs. Appreciation

International interest can feel flattering, until it doesn't.

Fetishization:

- Viewing you as a stereotype or novelty (e.g., "exotic Black woman") rather than a whole person.

- Comments focused on your race or body in a demeaning or reducing way.

Appreciation:

- Respectful admiration for your culture, personality, or achievements.
- Genuine curiosity about your story, rather than assumptions.

Boundary Tips:

- Politely redirect comments that feel objectifying.
- Share when you feel demeaned; assert boundaries calmly but firmly.

Cross-Cultural Communication

To connect deeply, you need emotional intelligence and cultural sensitivity:

- **Listen Actively:** Pay attention to nonverbal cues and indirect messaging.
- **Ask Open-Ended Questions:** Invite stories rather than yes/no answers.
- **Clarify and Reflect:** "I want to ensure I understand you correctly..."
- **Respect Silence:** In many cultures, pausing is thoughtful, not uncomfortable.

Patience and humility go a long way in bridging cultural gaps.

* * *

Romantic Relationships, Friendships, and Chosen Family Abroad

Romantic Relationships:

- Set clear expectations about commitment, timelines, and plans.

- Discuss cultural differences around finances, family roles, and gender dynamics early.

Friendships:

- Seek both expat and local friends for balanced perspectives.
- Invest time in one-on-one coffee dates, group outings, and shared projects.

Chosen Family:

- Cultivate a support network that feels like home: mentors, peers, and heart-based cohorts.
- Celebrate milestones together: birthdays, holidays, and personal achievements.

* * *

Love That Honors Your Liberation

Your relationships should elevate, not diminish, your freedom.

- **Mutual Growth:** Partners and friends who encourage your dreams, rest, and evolution.
- **Emotional Safety:** Spaces where your vulnerability is met with care, not criticism.
- **Autonomy:** The freedom to have time, voice, and vision.
- **Shared Values:** Alignment around honesty, consent, and personal sovereignty.

While many of us are moving abroad with partners or spouses, those of us who are single may find it's time to broaden the dating pool, and perhaps even the definition of what love can look like. My Nana always told me, "Fall in love with the one who's in love with you, not just the one you're in love with."

And it's true: there are people worldwide, Black men and women, and people across every identity, capable of loving you with tenderness, presence, and purpose.

There is someone out there who will allow you to be soft. Who will nurture and protect your heart without asking you to shrink or prove your worth?

I've witnessed women find deep, fulfilling love abroad, some within their ethnic community, others in places they never expected. The common thread? They permitted themselves to receive the love they deserved, not just the love they were conditioned to expect.

So, whether you find a connection with a man, woman, or someone beyond those boxes, remember: you are not here to perform. You are not here to settle. You are here to be cherished.

Love abroad is less about chasing romance and more about **creating a connection that honors your journey**, the healed, resting, and fully awakened versions of yourself.

* * *

Safety Considerations in Dating Abroad

- Always meet in public spaces until you know the person well.
- Share your location with a trusted friend before a date.
- Be cautious when sharing your home address early on.
- Understand local consent laws and cultural expectations around relationships.

Popular Platforms for Expats

- Tinder – Global, but approach with caution; can be hookup-focused.
- Bumble – Women message first; available in many countries.
- OKCupid – Detailed profiles are better for serious dating in some regions.
- InterNations & Meetup – These are not dating apps, but great for meeting singles in social groups.
- Facebook Expat & Hobby – Groups are Good for organic connections that can lead to dating.

Dating Cultural Etiquette Reminders

- In some cultures, physical affection in public may be frowned upon.
- Family involvement in dating is common; be prepared for more community interest in your relationship.
- Gender roles and dating "pace" can vary widely; observe before assuming.

* * *

Friendships and Chosen Family Abroad

Truthfully, while I've traveled extensively outside the United States, visiting different countries and soaking up new cultures, I've only lived long-term as a resident in one city and one country. From that experience, I learned something important: what you see in one part of a country doesn't always reflect the whole.

When planning my move, I based my decision on research I'd done about one specific city. But I didn't end up living in that city; I chose another. I assumed the expat community, energy, and support would be similar. Whew... I was so many levels wrong.

The city I moved to had an expat scene, but it was segregated. And the visible Black expat presence? It seemed more focused on aesthetics and flexing luxury lifestyles than building genuine community. There were no gatherings to help newcomers integrate or connect with local people. There were no cultural exchanges, shared meals, or guidance. There were occasional parties, surface-level conversations, and too many folks wrapped up in gossip, cliques, and comparisons. The kumbaya I imagined was nonexistent.

Most people like me, quietly living, healing, and building something real, were only visible at the grocery store or on the occasional Facebook post. We weren't looking to be seen for the sake of attention; we were seeking something deeper, something freer.

Now, I've heard similar stories from other Black women around the world: how they've approached someone they recognized as a fellow expat, same accent, same background, only to be ignored, dismissed, or outright avoided. It stings. But if I'm going to prepare you for this journey, I have to tell the whole truth: the good, the beautiful, the disappointing.

And let me be clear: I'm a NYC girl. I know how to move solo. But I'd be lying if I said it didn't catch me off guard to feel a lack of unity among my own people, within my current location abroad. So I'll tell you what I wish someone had told me: do your homework beyond the visa requirements. Don't just research where you want to live; research who lives there.

Check out local groups and events. Are the meetups focused on community, support, or cultural immersion? Do they include volunteering, family-friendly activities, or ways to connect with your host country? Or are they just parties and IG-worthy brunches?

Most importantly, don't judge the whole country by the vibe of one city or encounter. One cold shoulder shouldn't define your entire experience. I've been met with stank faces and side-eyes... and still love my city. Why? Because I stopped waiting for a community to show up for me, and I built my own.

My circle now includes Americans, folks from around the globe, and some of the kindest locals I've ever met. They've become my chosen family. And that is what sustains you more than beach photos or status updates.

* * *

Dating Safety Checklist

- Meet in public places.
- Share your location with a friend.
- Watch for financial or visa-related red flags.
- Leave if your gut says something is off.
- Keep personal documents private.

Reflection Prompts:

- What qualities are non-negotiable in my relationships abroad?
- How can I communicate my needs and boundaries with clarity and grace?
- Who in my life already reflects the love I want to receive and give?
- Am I open to love that looks different from what I imagined, but feels exactly right?

May every handshake, hug, and kiss remind you that you can love on your own terms.

Chapter 10: Safety, Boundaries & Thriving on Your Own Terms

Safety is not optional. Neither is your sanity.

Moving abroad is liberating but not risk-free. This chapter equips you with strategies to protect your body, mind, and spirit to live entirely without fear.

Emotional and Physical Self-Protection

Situational Awareness:

- Learn local emergency numbers and embassy contacts.
- Memorize key phrases: "Help," "Stop," "Call the police."
- Keep your phone charged, and share your location with trusted contacts.

Self-Care Essentials:

- Establish regular check-ins with a therapist or coach (virtual or local).
- Use grounding techniques: breathwork, meditation, or moments of mindful silence.
- Keep a personal safety kit: first-aid, basic medications, a power bank, and a backup ID.

Boundary-Setting in New Environments

Personal Boundaries:

- Practice saying "no" without over-explaining; you owe no one a justification for your limits.
- Use body language: maintain comfortable personal space, make eye contact, and speak clearly.

Digital Boundaries:

- Limit oversharing your location or routine on social media.
- Use secure apps and VPNs for communication and banking.

Social Boundaries:

- Decline invitations that don't align with your comfort or values.
- Set clear expectations for roommates or house cleaners regarding privacy and responsibilities.

* * *

Navigating Racism, Sexism, and Microaggressions Abroad

Prejudice can follow you no matter where you go, though its form may differ.

Strategies for Response:

- Direct but Safe: Calmly name what happened: "That comment felt disrespectful to me."
- Redirect: Change the topic or remove yourself from the situation.
- Seek Support: Discuss incidents with local allies or online support groups.

Vendor & Service Context:

- Minor slights may not be worth confrontation; focus on your overall network of safe relationships.
- Document incidents and seek legal advice for severe discrimination (employment, housing).

Minor slights may not be worth confrontation; focus on your overall network of safe relationships. Document incidents and seek legal advice for severe discrimination (employment, housing).

* * *

Protecting Your Peace While Living Fully

Thriving abroad requires choosing where to invest your energy.

Moving abroad isn't just about location; it's about liberation. But true liberation doesn't happen automatically. It requires intentional protection of your energy, peace, and presence. Even in paradise, toxicity can follow you if you let it.

Energy Audits

- Each week, take stock of what is nourishing you versus draining you.
- What relationships, conversations, habits, or digital routines steal your peace?
- Gradually release what no longer serves the woman you're becoming.

Sacred Downtime

- Build "white space" into your calendar. No plans. No output. Just restoration.
- Rest is not a luxury; it is a requirement for expansion.
- Your stillness is a radical refusal of hustle culture and over-functioning.

Digital Detox Is Self-Care

Something I failed at miserably in the beginning was protecting my peace. I had done the hard part—left the U.S., relocated to beauty, but I was still inviting the trauma in through my phone.

Every time I opened social media, I was hit with another wave of police brutality, American politics, anti- Blackness, and toxic commentary about Black women. The very place I had left was still inside me, through a screen.

I have a few social media theme pages, so logging off entirely wasn't possible. But I had to find boundaries. Because how could I be surrounded by beauty and still feel so poisoned?

You should choose digital spaces the same way you choose your home: with intention, care, and deep respect for your nervous system.

* * *

Family Fear and Freedom Guilt

Let's talk about family. Well-meaning, uninformed, and sometimes just afraid family.

Don't let people who've never owned a passport convince you that the rest of the world is more dangerous than the country you just left.

Some will try to scare you:
    "Isn't it dangerous over there?"
    "They don't like Black people anywhere."
    "At least here you know what you're dealing with."

After six months abroad, you'll start questioning everything you were taught to fear. You'll realize how deeply we've been conditioned to believe that chaos, hyper vigilance, and constant threat are everyday.

They're not.

After years of anxiety and medications like Prozac and Xanax, I haven't needed anti-anxiety meds in over four years abroad. But when I return to visit, I ask for a small prescription, because my nerves are completely done within days. My peace is under attack. My body remembers what it took to survive in a system built to wear us down.

Trust your own experience, not their fear or limitations. You didn't move away from your people; you moved toward your peace.

Thriving, Not Just Surviving

Freedom isn't just about escaping harm. It's about flourishing, creatively, socially, and spiritually.

- **Continuous Growth:** Mentor other expats, contribute to local communities, or start something of your own.
- **Give Back:** Take local classes, learn a new craft, or deepen a spiritual practice.
- **Celebrate Milestones:** Mark the dates you left, the days you chose yourself, and every moment you honored your evolution.

* * *

Your Expat Safety Toolkit

Apps

- Google Maps (offline maps downloaded)
- WhatsApp (primary communication in many countries)
- WhatsApp Live Location
- SmartTraveler (U.S. State Dept alerts)
- Red Panic Button or Noonlights (emergency alerts)

Contacts

- Local embassy/consulate phone number
- Two Trusted local friends or contacts you can call at any hour.
- Local emergency number (not always 911)
- Primary care doctor or clinic number

Habits

- Keep a charged power bank in your bag.
- Carry a small amount of local currency.
- Learn key phrases in the local language for emergencies.
- Trust your instincts, leave situations that feel unsafe.

Reflection Prompts:

- What energy leaks am I ready to seal?
- Who or what triggers survival-mode thinking in me, even from a distance?
- What does thriving feel like in my body?
- Am I permitting myself to rest without guilt?

You are not here to escape. You are here to expand.

Safety and boundaries aren't the opposite of adventure; they're the foundation it stands on. With them in place, you can soar, explore, and truly live on your own terms.

Chapter 11: Move Abroad and Enjoy the Good Life

Retirement is not an end. It's a rebirth. Whether you're seeking beach towns, art cities, or peaceful mountain villages, this chapter gives you the tools to retire abroad without breaking the bank.

Where Your Dollars Stretch Further

In many low- to mid-income countries, $2,000 a month can secure a comfortable lifestyle:

Destination	Rent (1BR)	Utilities	Food & Dining	Healthcare	Transportation	Total Estimate
Cuenca, Ecuador	$400	$50	$200	$30	$30	$720
Chiang Mai, Thailand	$350	$50	$150	$40	$20	$610
Morelia, Mexico	$360	$50	$180	$35	$25	$590
Abruzzo, Italy	$600	$100	$250	$50	40	$1,040
Languedoc, France	$650	$120	$300	$60	$50	$1,180

Affordable Healthcare That Respects Your Dignity

- Public Systems: Countries like Portugal and Costa Rica offer universal coverage for residents.
- Private Insurance: International plans can start as low as $50/month, covering outpatient and inpatient care
- Medical Tourism: For elective procedures (dental, vision, elective surgery), research trusted hospitals offering packages at a fraction of U.S. costs.

Key Tip: Verify whether your plan pays providers directly or requires upfront payment and reimbursement.

* * *

Renting vs. Owning

Renting Pros:

- Flexibility to relocate after a year
- No enormous upfront costs, property taxes, or maintenance

Renting Cons:

- Housing costs can rise annually.
- No asset accumulation

Owning Pros:

- Potential investment appreciation
- Stability and personalization of your living space

Owning Cons:

- Significant upfront investment or mortgage
- Ongoing maintenance and property taxes

Strategy: Rent for your first 6–12 months abroad to ensure the area fits your lifestyle. Then evaluate purchasing based on long-term plans and local real estate market conditions.

> **Voices From Abroad – Sade in Portugal**
>
> "I wake up in Porto to the sound of church bells, not traffic. My morning coffee is at a café where the barista knows my name. I work remotely until lunch, then walk to the market for fresh produce. Evenings are for meeting friends by the river. My rent is half what

I paid in Chicago, and I've swapped my commute for daily walks."

Budget Planning for Joy, Not Just Survival

- **Essential Expenses:** Rent, utilities, food, healthcare, Transportation, Insurance
- **Joy Budget:** Allocate at least 10–15% of your monthly spending to leisure spa treatments, cultural events, and travel days.
- **Emergency Cushion:** Maintain a 3–6 month reserve in local or USD-denominated accounts.

Sample Monthly Breakdown (Total $1,500):

- Housing & Utilities: $650
- Food & Transportation: $350
- Healthcare & Insurance: $100.
- Miscellaneous / Bills: $200
- Joy Budget: $150
- Savings / Emergency Fund: $50

Living Soft, Slow, and Sacred

Your relocation should be defined by ease and enchantment:

- **Slow Mornings:** Sunrise walks, journaling, or gentle yoga.
- **Sacred Spaces:** Create a cozy corner with local art and plants.
- **Community Rituals:** Join local clubs for dance, art, or language exchange.
- **Mindful Moments:** Pause mid-day for tea, reading, or silent reflection.

These practices honor the spirit of retirement as a time to savor life, not just endure it.

Voices From Abroad – Darren in Thailand

"In Chiang Mai, my days are slower. Breakfast is tropical fruit from the market, followed by a few hours of consulting work. Afternoons might be a Thai class or a $7 massage. Weekends mean short trips to temples or waterfalls. My monthly expenses are under $1,000, and I've met more people in six months here than in five years back home."

* * *

Tax Considerations: Navigating Double Filing and Avoiding Pitfalls

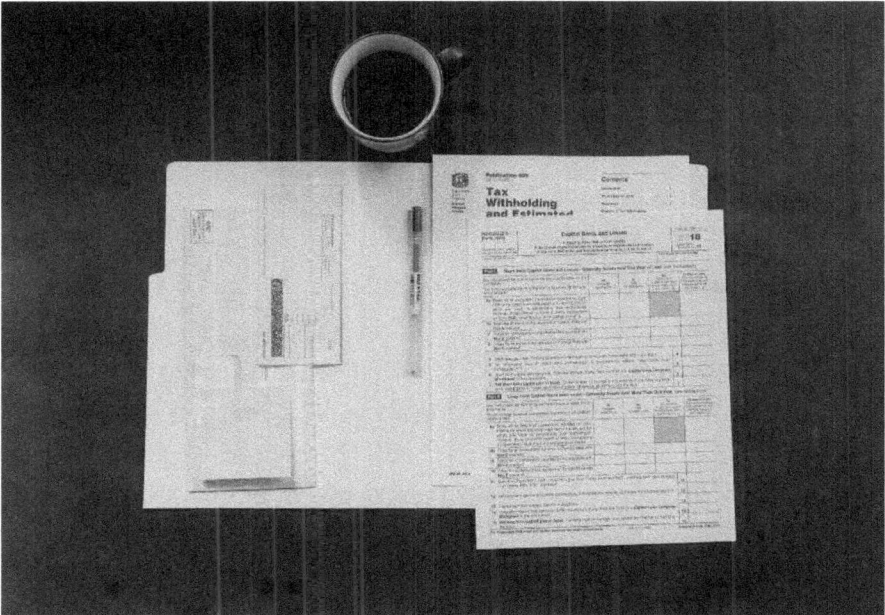

Smart Money Moves Abroad

Moving abroad isn't just about palm trees and cheaper rent; you're also entering a new financial landscape. Here's how to keep your money safe, growing, and working for you regardless of zip code.

Maximize Your U.S. Tax Benefits

The IRS doesn't care where you live. As a U.S. citizen, you must file taxes yearly, even if you never set foot in America. But there are ways to reduce or even eliminate your U.S. tax bill legally.

What is FEIE (Foreign Earned Income Exclusion)?

The Foreign Earned Income Exclusion lets you exclude up to $126,500 (2024 limit) of earned income (wages or self-employment) from your U.S. taxes if you meet the requirements.

You must pass either:

- **330 Day Test** – You're physically outside the U.S. for 330 full days in 12 months.
- **Bona Fide Residence Test** – You're a resident of a foreign country for a full calendar year with proof of ties (lease, utility bills, local taxes)

⚠ *FEIE applies to earned income only, not retirement pensions, Social Security, rental income, or investments.*

What is the FTC (Foreign Tax Credit)?

- If you pay taxes to your host country, you can claim a dollar-for-dollar credit on your U.S. tax return to avoid double taxation.

- This is clutch for folks with investment income, pensions, or anything over the FEIE limit.

Pro Tip: Even if you qualify for FEIE or FTC, you must file your U.S. return yearly. Skipping it can cause significant headaches later (and cost you thousands).

Sample Scenarios:

Freelancer earning $80K remotely in Portugal:

- Qualifies for FEIE → Excludes all $80K from U.S. tax if meeting residency test.
- They still may owe Portuguese taxes, but they can offset them using the FTC if double-taxed.

Retiree living off Social Security in Mexico:

- Social Security is generally not taxed by Mexico (due to a treaty), but you still report it to the IRS.
- No FEIE benefit here because Social Security is not "earned income."

Avoid Banking Pitfalls

Why expats' U.S. bank accounts sometimes get frozen:

- Banks flag logins from foreign IP addresses as potential fraud.
- Prolonged absence can trigger "inactivity" rules.
- Some banks close accounts if they suspect you're no longer a U.S. resident.

How to set up global-friendly banking:

- **Wise** – Multi-currency accounts, low transfer fees, local bank details in multiple countries.

- **Revolut** – Holds multiple currencies, instant exchange at interbank rates, and is excellent for travel spending.
- **Charles Schwab High Yield Investor Checking** – No foreign ATM fees and unlimited global ATM fee reimbursements.

Using digital wallets & fintech:

- **PayPal and Payoneer** are ideal for receiving freelance payments.
- **Venmo, Cash App** – Limited use abroad (U.S. only for sending/receiving), but can link to your U.S. bank for withdrawals.
- **Apple Pay / Google Pay** – Works in many countries if your bank card supports it.

Keep a U.S. mailing address (family, trusted friend, or virtual mailbox)

Virtual Mailbox Cost Comparison (Estimated Monthly Fees)

Service	Basic Plan Cost*	Scanning + Forwarding	Address Locations/U.S. States	Optional Extras
Anytime Mailbox	$10 - 15	Several scans, pay-per-forward	Many U.S. states, street addresses	App alerts, multiple users
VirtualPostMail (VPM)	$15 - 20	More frequent scans + free scans included	Addresses in a few big cities	Check deposits, package forwarding
iPoststal1	$14 -18	Included scans + forwarding at extra cost	Lots of U.S. address options	Premium address, extra users
US Global Mail	$25 - 30	Higher scan quota + forwarding	Main U.S. metros	Package consolidation, check deposits

*Prices approximate for basic plans. Extras (scanning, forwarding, premium addresses) often cost more.

Tip: Have two accounts... one U.S. and one local. Keep enough in both so that if one freezes, you're still eating.

You **do not** want to be stuck abroad with a frozen U.S. bank account because your bank "detected suspicious foreign activity."

Checklist: What to Ask Before Choosing a Virtual Mailbox Service

1. **Address Type**—Is it a "street address" or a P.O. Box? Some banks only accept street addresses.
2. **Bank Acceptance** - Will banks accept this address to open/maintain accounts and avoid "residency concerns"?
3. **Scanning Frequency & Cost:** How many scans are included per month, and what's the fee for extra scans?
4. **Forwarding Fees** - How much to forward physical mail or packages overseas?
5. **Package Handling** - Do they accept packages? Do they consolidate or charge per package?
6. **Check Deposit** - Can you deposit U.S. checks via the service?
7. **Security & Privacy** - What security features are in place? How is your mail stored, and how are images handled?
8. **Customer Service** - Is support fast and responsive? Are there phone/e-mail/online chat options?
9. **Pricing Structure** - Are there extra fees (set-up, monthly, scanning, forwarding, storage)?
10. **Trial or Refund Policy:** Do they let you try before fully committing? Is there a refund if you are unsatisfied?

* * *

Protecting Your Assets from Afar

LLCs and trusts for real estate and investments:

- Holding U.S. rental property in an LLC can protect your personal assets from lawsuits.
- Trusts can help manage inheritance and avoid probate, especially if you own property in multiple countries.

What happens to your U.S.-based assets when you live abroad:

- You still have U.S. legal and tax obligations on U.S.-based property and investments.
- Rental income is taxable in the U.S. and potentially in your host country (check treaties)..

Insurance, wills, and expat estate planning:

- Update your will to reflect your new country's laws; some nations don't honor U.S. wills.
- Consider an international term life insurance policy that covers you regardless of country.
- Review your health insurance; many U.S.-based policies don't cover you abroad for extended stays.

If you plan to live abroad long-term, get an estate plan that works internationally. Yes, it costs money now, but it can save your family a fortune later.

* * *

FEIE Cheat Sheet — Foreign Earned Income Exclusion

(For U.S. Citizens Living Abroad)

What It Is:

The Foreign Earned Income Exclusion (FEIE) lets you exclude up to $126,500 of foreign-earned income from U.S. taxes in 2024 (adjusted annually).

Who Qualifies?

You must meet **all** three requirements:

Foreign Earned Income

- Money earned from work outside the U.S. (wages, salaries, freelance income).
- **Not Included:** passive income like dividends, rental income, pensions, and Social Security.

Tax Home Abroad

- Your principal place of business, employment, or post is in a foreign country.

One of Two Tests:

- Bona Fide Residence Test: You must have lived in a foreign country for an uninterrupted **full calendar year** (Jan–Dec).
- Physical Presence Test: You've been outside the U.S. for **330 full** calendar days in 12 months.

* * *

How to Claim It

File Form 2555 with your annual U.S. tax return (Form 1040).

Keep records of:

- Entry/exit dates (passport stamps, flight receipts).
- Foreign addresses & employment contracts.
- Proof of income earned abroad.

* * *

Example Scenarios
Example 1 — Freelancer in Portugal

- Earns: $80,000/year
- Lives abroad full-time (Physical Presence Test met).
- It can exclude the full $80,000, but there is no U.S. federal tax on that income.

Example 2 — Digital Marketer in Thailand

- Earns: $95,000/year from U.S. and international clients.
- Lives abroad full-time and spends fewer than 20 days in the U.S. yearly (Physical Presence Test met).
- You can exclude the full $95,000; there is no U.S. federal tax on that income (but you are still responsible for self-employment tax unless you use a business structure to reduce it).

Example 3 — ESL Teacher in Bali (Part-Time Resident)

Earns: $45,000/year teaching English online to students worldwide.

- **Lives abroad 7 months/year** and spends the remaining 5 months in the U.S. (Does not meet the Physical Presence Test for FEIE).

Can still qualify for a partial FEIE exclusion by prorating the amount based on days spent abroad.

- 17 months abroad = ~210 days/365 days = **57% of income eligible** for exclusion.
- 45,000 × 57% = $25,650 excluded from U.S. federal taxes.
- The rest ($19,350) is taxed as regular U.S. income.

Example 4 — Retiree in Mexico

Lives abroad full-time.

- Income is from Social Security + U.S. retirement accounts.
- FEIE doesn't apply, but FEIE may benefit from the non-automatic **Foreign Tax Credit** instead.

Tips:

- FEIE is, but you may benefit from the **non-automatic** Foreign Tax Credit; you must claim it each year
- FEIE doesn't exempt you from **self-employment tax**; consider forming a business entity abroad to reduce that.
- Combine **FEIE + Foreign Tax Credit** for maximum savings if you pay taxes in your host country.
- Don't break your foreign residency accidentally by spending too many days in the U.S.

Reminder:

Your peace of mind abroad isn't just about knowing where the best coffee is; it's about understanding your money is untouchable, your income streams are diversified, and your family is protected no matter what. Whether you're on a hammock in Costa Rica or a terrace in Italy, the government isn't going to remind you to protect your money. That's your job. Stay informed, keep receipts, and *never let one paycheck, bank account, or country be the only thing between you and your financial freedom.*

Chapter 12: Your First 90 Days Abroad

This isn't a vacation. It's the start of your new life.

Those first three months in a new country are magical and messy. They mix fresh starts and foreign systems, beauty and bureaucracy, awe and adaptation. This chapter is your 90-day guide to landing softly, rooting deeply, and staying the course with clarity, confidence, and care.

Phase 1: Weeks 1-2 — Orientation & Grounding

You've arrived. Breathe. It's okay if everything feels surreal.

Focus on:

- **Getting settled:** unpack, walk the neighborhood, find your grocery store, coffee spot, and pharmacy.
- **Navigating Logistics:** SIM card, local transportation card, internet setup, plug adaptors.
- **Sleeping well:** Prioritise Rest and hydration; jet lag and cultural shift fatigue are real.
- **Initial registrations:** address visa check-ins, tourist card validation, or temporary residency stamps.
- **Take notes:** Write down what feels unfamiliar, what sparks joy, and what frustrates you. You'll need this reflection later.

Emotional check-in: You may feel exhilarated... or unbothered. Both are normal.

* * *

Phase 2: Weeks 3-6 — Integration & Observation

Now the novelty fades a little, and the real learning begins.

Focus on:

- **Language basics:** learn how to greet people, ask for help, order food, and give directions in the local language
- **Observe social customs:** when do people eat? How do they dress? What's

considered polite?
- **You can meet people by** attending a language exchange, finding a Black expat meetup, or joining a co-working or parenting group.
- **Research healthcare:** find a local doctor, understand your nearest hospital options, and fill prescriptions
- **Track expenses:** document daily spending and compare it to your projected budget.
- **Identify** safe walking routes and transportation options.

Emotional check-in: This is where culture shock often shows up. You might feel isolated or overly critical. Pause. Breathe. You're still adjusting and doing beautifully.

* * *

Phase 3: Weeks 7-12 — Rhythms & Rebuilding

By now, you've had some wins and some setbacks. Now it's time to rebuild routines that anchor you.

Focus on:

- **Design your lifestyle:** What does your ideal week look like here? Add soft structure: market day, walking day, reading day, social day.
- **Start small traditions:** Sunday dinner with a new friend, solo café mornings, Friday art strolls.
- **Explore deeper:** visit nearby towns, museums, or natural sites, and go beyond the tourist path.
- **Handle admin:** renew short-term visas if needed, apply for longer-term residency, update insurance info.
- **Map your comfort zone:** find your "go-to" doctor, café, mechanic, and taxi service.

- **Begin planning the following steps:** Emotional check-in: Will you stay longer? Will you move cities? Will you switch visas? Will you travel again?

Emotional check-in: You're no longer just in your new home but part of it. Celebrate that.

Pro Tips for a Smooth 90 Days

- **Permit yourself to slow down.** You're not behind. You're adapting.
- **Make one local friend**—just one—someone who can help you decode systems, slang, or cultural cues.
- **Document the journey.** Journals, voice notes, and photo logs will become powerful mirrors of your growth.
- **Don't rush to fix discomfort.** Observe before acting. Reaction is not always integration.
- **Celebrate small wins.** Every document submitted, every local phrase mastered, every day you don't feel lost is a win.

* * *

A Note on Safety and Sanity

- **Emergency plan:** Know how to contact emergency services in your new country. Learn a few emergency phrases in the local language.
- **Embassy registration:** Consider registering with your country's local consulate for updates and support.
- **Boundaries:** You don't owe anyone access to your space, time, or energy just because you're new.
- **Rest. Often.** You are living in a new language, culture, and rhythm. That's a full-time, energetic job in itself.

* * *

Your First 90 Days Aren't About Perfection — They're About Permission.

This is permission to feel lost and still be brave, get it wrong and try again, and take up space with humility, respect, and curiosity.

You're not just surviving. You're becoming someone who knows how to belong anywhere.

Chapter 13: Mistakes That Cost You — and How to Avoid Them

Moving abroad is exciting and liberating. But excitement can cloud judgment, and the stakes are too high to wing it. This chapter discusses expats' most common (and costly) mistakes and how to avoid them.

Underestimating the Cost of Living

The Trap: A blog post says you can live in Bali for $900/month. It doesn't say that the estimate assumes you don't eat out, drive, or get sick.

The Fix:

- **Always use a conservative budget.** Add 20–30% cushion for unexpected expenses (visa renewal fees, appliance repairs, seasonal rent hikes).
- **Ask multiple expats living in the area what they actually spend.**
- Track every expense for the first three months to adjust your projections in real time.

Overspending in "Vacation Mode"

The Trap: You arrive in your new country, and suddenly, every day feels like a holiday, with new restaurants, excursions, and upgrades. Before you know it, you're living beyond your means.

The Fix:

- **Set a lifestyle budget before you land**, and stick to it.
- **Differentiate between settling in and splurging.** Yes, explore, but also anchor into daily rhythms and routines.
- **Automate savings** to prevent draining your funds on impulse buys.

Not Using Local Experts

The Trap: Trying to DIY your way through everything, from real estate to legal documents, using only English-language Google searches and American logic.

The Fix:

- **Hire local professionals:** real estate agents, lawyers, tax consultants, translators.
- **Pay for wisdom, not just labor.** A $100 consult today could save you thousands in fines, missed tax credits, or shady property deals.
- **Trust cultural fluency over assumptions.** Just because it's done one way in the U.S. doesn't mean it's done that way abroad.

Not Updating Your Will or Estate Plan

The Trap: You move abroad with an estate plan made for your home country, only to find that local laws don't recognize it.

The Fix:

- **Draft a local will in your new country** to cover any property or assets acquired abroad.
- **Review inheritance and property laws** (some countries automatically pass assets to children or the state).
- **Consult with estate attorneys in both countries if you're a dual resident.**

Currency Conversion Traps

The Trap: Thinking of money in U.S. dollars without accounting for fluctuations, fees, or exchange rates.

The Fix:

- **Use multi-currency accounts** (like Wise, Revolut, or Charles Schwab) that allow local transactions and minimize conversion fees.
- **Watch exchange rates** when moving large sums (like rental deposits or property purchases).
- **Avoid ATM cards or banks that charge international fees.** Choose accounts that refund those charges monthly.

Bonus Mistake: Not Having a Local Emergency Plan

The Trap: Believing nothing bad will happen just because everything feels good.

The Fix:

- Know where the nearest hospital, embassy, and emergency services are.
- Keep a "go bag" with documents, cash, copies of IDs, and contact lists.
- Share your location and emergency plan with loved ones in both countries.

Bottom Line

You don't have to be perfect. You have to be prepared. Every mistake above is avoidable; none should stop you from living boldly and beautifully abroad. Learn from others, check your blind spots, and build your new life from a place of clarity and care.

Dollar Impact of Common Moving Abroad Mistakes

Mistake	Example Scenario	Potential Cost
Not Checking Visa Work Rights	Taking a local job on a tourist visa and being fined	$500–$2,000 + possible ban
Skipping Health Insurance	Emergency surgery abroad	$8,000–$25,000
Poor Currency Planning	Using a U.S. bank card with foreign transaction fees	$300–$800/year
Not Confirming Housing Before Arrival	Staying in hotels for weeks while searching	$1,000–$3,000
Skipping Everything	Paying for freight + customs instead of buying local	$2,000–$5,000
Rental Scam	You wire money for an apartment you found online. When you arrive, the property doesn't exist or is already rented	$500–$2,000 lost in deposits and fees
Wrong Visa Choice	You apply for a short-term tourist visa when you actually qualify for a long-stay residency. You're forced to leave and reapply.	$5,000+ in extra flights, penalties, and new applications
Skipping Healthcare	You decide not to buy international health insurance. After an accident or illness, you pay out-of-pocket.	$10,000+ in unexpected medical bills
Bad Business Contract	You sign a lease or partnership agreement without legal review. Hidden clauses or disputes force you out of the deal.	$50,000+ in losses, legal fees, or unrecoverable investments

Mistake-Proof Moving Abroad: Your Checklist

Before You Move:

- Build a conservative monthly budget with a 30% buffer.
- Research realistic local costs (ask at least three expats)
- Meet with an international tax advisor.
- Hire a local real estate agent or legal consultant.
- Draft or update your will to comply with local laws
- Open a multi-currency account or a fee-free international banking solution.

- Convert emergency funds into the local currency.
- Create a local emergency plan (contacts, hospitals, embassy)

After You Arrive:

- Track your expenses for the first 90 days.
- Set up your daily/weekly routine (don't float in vacation mode)
- Build a relationship with a local fixer, lawyer, or translator.
- Get familiar with currency conversion tools and real-time rates.
- Create a "go bag" with essentials and backup IDs.
- Join an expat or international community group for support

Costly Mistakes vs. Smart Moves

Costly Mistake	Smart Move
Budgeting off blog estimates	Building a 20–30% cushion in your monthly budget
Partying like it's a two-year vacation	Living soft, slow, and intentional — from day one
DIYing legal, real estate, or taxes	Paying for local expert guidance upfront
Using U.S.-only bank accounts abroad	Opening a fee-free multicurrency or global ATM account
Relying on your U.S. will alone	Drafting a will valid in your new
Thinking "it'll be ne" in an emergency	Having a local emergency plan with key contacts ready

Reflections

- Think about a time you rushed into something without doing enough research. What cost you (time, money, peace of mind)?
- Which mistake from this chapter feels most likely to you: rental scams, visa errors, skipping health insurance, or bad contracts? Why?
- What systems or habits do you need to set up now to protect yourself

from these mistakes (e.g., budgeting tools, legal help, or a mentor)?

- How do you usually respond when things go wrong: panic, denial, or problem-solving? How can you build a calmer, more prepared response?
- If you did make one of these costly mistakes abroad, who could you lean on for support?

Affirmations

- I prepare with intention so I don't pay the price of rushing.
- I respect my money, my time, and my peace.
- I double-check the details because my freedom is worth it.
- I learn from mistakes instead of letting them define me.
- I trust myself to ask for help when I need it.
- I am building a safe, secure foundation for my life abroad.

Chapter 14: Building a Location-Independent Life Long- Term

Freedom isn't a vacation — it's a lifestyle.

Moving abroad isn't the end of your journey; it's the beginning of a new way of living. For many, relocation is the first chapter in a life built on self-determination, mobility, and intentionality. But how do you create a location-independent life that works financially, emotionally, legally, and logistically over time?

This chapter is your blueprint for sustainability and sovereignty abroad.

What Is a Location Independent Life?

Being location independent means you are not tied to one city, country, or traditional office to live and earn. It's the ability to choose where and how you live, whether you stay in one peaceful town for a decade or move every six months.

It's not about always being on the move. It's about being able to move on your own terms.

* * *

Key Pillars of Long-Term Freedom Abroad

1. Financial Sustainability

Diversify your income streams:

- **Remote jobs** (customer support, marketing, writing, tech, education)
- **Freelancing** (design, consulting, virtual assistance)
- **Passive income (**rental properties, digital products, dividends)
- **Online business** (coaching, e-commerce, courses)

Create a financial rhythm:

- **Set up separate savings:** emergency fund, relocation fund, and joy fund.
- **Use tools** like Wise, Payoneer, or Revolut for borderless banking.
- **Keep an eye on** currency exchange and inflation in your base country.

Protect your earning power:

- **Invest in skills** that travel well (language, coding, copywriting, teaching)
- **Build a client base** or audience you can serve from anywhere.
- **Get professional support** for taxes in both countries

Maintaining Income Streams Long-Term

- **Diversify Your Sources**—Don't rely on one client, employer, or platform. Maintain at least two active streams of income.
- **Invest in Skills** – Dedicate 5–10% of your monthly time or budget to learning new tools or certifications.
- **Protect Your Work Infrastructure** – Keep backups of files, maintain a strong VPN, and store passwords securely.
- **Adjust for Currency Shifts**—If your pay is in USD but you live abroad, monitor exchange rates and prepare for fluctuations.
- **Maintain a Professional Network** – Even if you're abroad, regularly connect with peers and clients via LinkedIn, Zoom, and industry events.
- **Plan for Downtime** – Save at least 3 months' living expenses to cover slow seasons or contract gaps.

* * *

2. Legal Stability
Choose the correct visas and residencies:

- **Digital nomad visas** (available in 40+ countries now)

- **Retirement visas** with low income requirements
- **Residency t**hrough property investment or income proof, Long-stay student, or self-employment visas

Strategic base-building:

Consider countries with flexible long-term paths to residency or dual citizenship (e.g., Mexico, Portugal, Panama, Uruguay).

Protect your identity and rights abroad:

- **Keep** multiple forms of ID.
- **Have** cloud backups of passports, banking info, and legal docs
- **Understand** local legal rights as a renter, worker, or resident.

* * *

3. Emotional Anchoring

This is where many digital nomads fail. Freedom isn't just logistics; it's emotional intelligence in motion.

Make space for structure:

- **Create routines,** even when changing locations.
- **Build daily rituals** that bring peace and grounding.
- **Design** a "mobile home" lifestyle, your comfort doesn't need a zip code

Stay connected:

- Join expat networks, coworking communities, or online support circles.
- Schedule regular calls with loved ones at home.

- Build friendships slowly and intentionally in each place you live

4. Health & Insurance

Don't skip this. Health emergencies abroad can derail your lifestyle fast.

- Enroll in long-term international health insurance or a global expat plan.
- Understand local healthcare access and quality where you stay.
- Know the nearest hospitals, clinics, and emergency protocols.
- Prioritize mental health just as much as physical care

5. Reassess Often

Freedom evolves. What worked last year might not fit anymore.

Every 6–12 months, ask:

- Does my current base still feel aligned with my goals?
- Is my income model sustainable and joyful?
- What's missing from my life right now?
- What am I tolerating that I no longer need to?

* * *

Long-Term Stability Abroad

- Research tax obligations in your home and host countries. Keep building retirement savings through IRAs or international accounts.
- Register your business legally where you live.
- Diversify income so one client or platform can't sink you.

You're Not Just Escaping — You're Creating

A location-independent life isn't about outrunning discomfort. It's about choosing a reality that honors your wholeness. It's about building a soft, sovereign, and sustainable life that feels like yours.

Whether you stay planted in one country or drift between continents, you can design a life that fits you, not a passport, a paycheck, or anyone else's expectations.

Reflections

- What skills, knowledge, or talents do I already have that I could turn into income abroad?
- Am I relying on only one stream of income right now? How would my life change if that income stopped tomorrow?
- What fears arise when considering working for myself or earning money outside the U.S./U.K.?
- What does financial freedom *look like* for me abroad? Is it less stress, more time, or more choices?
- Who can I learn from or collaborate with to strengthen my income plan?
- How can I make my money work multiple ways instead of only trading hours for pay?

Affirmations

- I am not limited to one way of earning or living.
- My skills and talents can support me anywhere in the world.
- I create income that matches my values and my freedom.
- I am building streams of money that flow even when I rest.
- I am adaptable, resourceful, and resilient.
- My financial independence supports my personal autonomy.

Chapter 15: Before You Go — Smart Tips & Tidbits

Details matter. Especially when crossing borders.

While dreaming, budgeting, and planning are essential parts of international relocation, they are often the overlooked details that cause the most stress once you arrive. This chapter is your last-minute logistics guide, the fine print that can make the difference between a smooth transition and a frustrating experience.

Use this chapter as your pre-departure checklist to ensure you're ready to leave and land well.

Driver's Licenses Abroad

- Renew your U.S. driver's license before departure. Some states make renewals difficult if you no longer have a U.S. address.
- Apply for an International Driving Permit (IDP). Valid in over 150 countries, it's often required if you're driving abroad on a tourist or temporary visa.
- Learn the rules in your destination country. Some countries allow driving with a U.S. license for a limited time (often 90 days), after which you must obtain a local permit.
- If you plan to purchase a car abroad, you may need a local license to register or insure the vehicle.

Cell Phone Logistics

- Unlock your U.S. phone before you go so you can use a local SIM card. Contact your carrier to unlock it if it's still under contract.
- Local prepaid SIM cards are often the cheapest way to get mobile service in your new country.
- Alternatively, consider an international eSIM (such as Google Fi or Airalo) if traveling between multiple countries.
- Use Wi-Fi-based apps like WhatsApp, Signal, Google Voice, or Telegram for international calls and messaging; these are standard communication tools abroad.

Rental Agreements and Real Estate Customs

Don't assume U.S. standards apply. In many countries:

- Rental homes may not include appliances, light fixtures, or even cabinet handles.

- Security deposits and lease terms can vary greatly. Please read the contract carefully and consider having it reviewed by a local expert.
- Outside major cities, handshake rental agreements are still standard. Avoid these if possible, always get terms in writing, even informally via email or text.

Buy only after living locally. It's wise to rent for 6 to 12 months before purchasing a property. This gives you time to explore neighborhoods and understand the real estate market.

Shipping vs. Rebuying

- Shipping personal items internationally can be costly and logistically complicated—research customs fees, import duties, and the cost of international freight before making any decisions.
- Compare replacement cost vs. shipping cost. For many items, such as large furniture or electronics, it may be cheaper and simpler to sell them before you move and buy new or used items once you are abroad.
- Appliances and electronics may be more expensive or less available in some countries. Research this ahead of time to avoid surprises.
- Use freight forwarders and expat shipping companies that understand destination country regulations and can help you avoid overpaying in taxes or fines.

Bonus Tips Before Departure

- Scan and store digital copies of your passport, visa documents, birth certificate, insurance cards, and key legal or financial paperwork. Save them securely online and on an external drive.
- Notify banks and credit card companies that you'll be abroad. Ask about international fees and which cards are most travel-friendly.
- Set up online bill pay for any recurring U.S. obligations.

- If you give up your U.S. residence, plan for mail forwarding through USPS or a virtual mailbox service.
- Bring extra passport-sized photos. Photos for applications.
- Start building your local network early. Join expat forums or Facebook groups in your destination country to ask questions, get referrals, and connect before you land.

Final 30 Days Countdown

- Cancel subscriptions and auto-payments. Set up mail forwarding.
- Notify your bank and credit card companies.
- Get health and dental checkups.
- Digitally back up all critical documents.

* * *

Final Departure Checklist

Documents

- Passport valid for at least 6 months
- Required visas approved
- Copies of IDs and birth certificates
- International health insurance policy

Finances

- Notify banks of travel dates.
- Set up online bill pay.
- Arrange access to emergency funds.

Housing

- End lease or sell property
- Forward mail
- Cancel or transfer utilities.

Health & Safety

- Get required vaccinations
- Refill prescriptions
- Record emergency contacts

Travel Prep

- Book temporary accommodation for arrival.
- Arrange airport pickup or transport.
- Download offline maps

Download a clean version of this checklist from the Resources section for easy printing.

Chapter 16: Being Black Abroad — Culture, Colorism & Feeling Free

There's a moment that hits many Black women after they've lived abroad for a while.

It doesn't arrive with fireworks. Some grand milestone doesn't mark it. It's quiet, sometimes subtle. But when it comes, it's unforgettable.

It's the moment you realize: you're **no longer shrinking.**

You walk down the street without clutching your keys. You exist in public space without being questioned or followed. You speak without code-switching and still feel heard. You smile at someone, and they smile back. There is no suspicion, no side-eye, no defensiveness, just humanity.

For the first time in a long time, maybe ever, you feel what it's like *just to be*.

You're not representing. You're not explaining. You're not defending your right to take up space. You're simply living.

Racism Doesn't Disappear—But It Shifts

> ## "I feel safer in my skin here."

Let's be clear: anti-Blackness exists everywhere. No country is entirely free from prejudice. But what changes is its form, and often, its weight.

In many countries, you're not seen as a threat. You're not seen through the lens of American policing, media-fueled fear, or generational trauma. In some places, you're exoticized. In others, invisible. But many Black expats, especially African American women, report a familiar, almost spiritual theme:

That doesn't mean racism vanishes. But the intensity of it, the hypervigilance it requires back home, can ease. You are still Black. But you are not constantly being punished for it.

That alone can change your entire nervous system.

Colorism and Texturism Still Exist

Beauty standards in Latin America, Asia, and Africa still favor lighter skin, thinner noses, and looser curls. You may encounter looks, comments, or advertising that reflect colonial ideals.

But here's what often feels different abroad:

- You are not into believing it doesn't exist.
- You are not asked to prove that it's real.
- You are not punished for naming it.

And in many places, you'll find local and expat communities actively reclaiming space for dark skin, kinkier textures, and fuller features. You get to choose your circles, affirm your beauty, and wear your crown without explaining why your hair "isn't unprofessional."

You are no longer in constant defense of your body. You are in celebration of it.

My Personal Experience: Finding Peace Abroad

One of the most significant shifts I felt after leaving the U.S. was the peace that came with not having to worry about police breathing down my neck for no reason. Back home, I always felt like I had to prove I belonged, wasn't a threat, or tone myself down to exist. Out here, that weight is gone.

I can walk into a store and be the only Black person there, and instead of side-eyes or suspicion, I get smiles. Babies try to chat with me. Nobody's following me. Nobody's waiting for me to slip something in my bag. The only attention I get is when I need customer service or help, and I get it without hesitation.

I also made it a point to learn people's names in my neighborhood: the woman who owns the dress shop, the sister running the restaurant down the block, her delivery driver, the convenience store clerks, my neighbors, and the barista who already knows my coffee order. Over time, these weren't just transactions. They became real connections.

I'll give you an example. I caught a cold from my friend's grandbaby. We kept passing it back and forth before realizing it was contagious. I decided to stay in the house so I wouldn't spread it around. After a few days, the dress shop owner called to check on me. She knew I usually ordered lunch from the local restaurant, and when I finally did, the delivery driver told me the meal had already been paid for.

The next day, the restaurant started including juice and teas with my order, at no extra charge. Then the nail spa owner called and gave me a home remedy

I'd never heard of, and it worked like magic.

That kind of care? I can't say it doesn't exist in the U.S., but outside of close friends or family, I never experienced that kind of community care back home. Nobody checked in on me like that, bringing me free food or ensuring I was okay.

Now, let me be real. Anti-Blackness exists everywhere. It hasn't disappeared where I live. But here, the way it shows up is different. At worst, it looks like not getting invited to a barbecue or not getting long conversations from certain people. And honestly, that's fine with me. I handle it the same way I do anywhere, respectfully, but distanced. No hard feelings, no need to force it. It's such a small part of life here that it barely registers, like bumping into a not-so-friendly person once or twice a year.

And sometimes, it might not even be about race. Where I live, if I don't open my mouth, people don't know if I'm a local or a foreigner. Especially outside my neighborhood, I blend in until I speak. That alone changes the way I'm treated day to day.

The one thing that does happen sometimes, especially on nights out, is interesting, funny, and sad all at once. People will send us drinks or stop by our table and say, "I'm so sorry your country treats your people that way," or something close to it. The first time it happened, I didn't know how to react. But over time, I realized it actually meant a lot. It felt good to know that people outside the U.S. *see* what's happening to Black and Brown folks back home. They recognize it. They acknowledge it. And that acknowledgment matters.

That's when I realized something important: safety isn't only about crime rates or policing. It's also about being seen, supported, and cared for. And in this community, I felt safe in a way I hadn't felt in years.

"Not every experience will look like mine, but what matters is finding where you feel safe and seen."

Blackness Without Performance

Living abroad gives you the rare and radical opportunity to redefine how you experience your Blackness.

While there are Black men who love us deeply, and we love and appreciate them too, many single Black women abroad report an unexpected relief: the weight of constant scrutiny lifts. The relentless conversations about our "undesirability," the attacks on our femininity, the ridicule for simply existing as we are—those voices fade into the background. You finally get just to be yourself—whole, worthy, unbothered.

In the U.S., your identity is often shaped in opposition to trauma:
  "resilient," "strong," "overcomer." These are survival terms, earned but heavy.

Abroad, you can begin to explore a new language of self:
  Curious. Rested. Soft. Creative. Loved.

You begin to experience joy that isn't framed by pain.
  You express your culture without being reduced to it.
  You create without having to represent an entire race.

You start to realize that your Blackness is not just a reaction to white supremacy. It is a universe. It is a culture. It is an inheritance, and it is allowed to breathe.

You might even meet parts of yourself you've never had space to uncover before.

The version of you that isn't always bracing.

The version of you that laughs louder. Rests deeper. Loves more freely.

The version of you that is finally, beautifully, at peace.

Reflection Prompts

- Where in my life have I felt most free in my skin?
- What does Black joy look like without struggle attached?
- What parts of my identity have I been holding too tightly, or hiding too often?
- What would it feel like to be seen, not just watched?
- Who do I become when I am no longer surviving?

Affirmations

- I deserve to live in spaces where my life is valued.
- My Blackness is not a burden; brilliance travels with me.
- I belong everywhere I choose to be.
- I release the fear of being targeted simply for existing.
- I am open to communities that see, respect, and welcome me.
- My presence is powerful, even in places where I am the only one.
- I create safety through boundaries, awareness, and self-respect.
- I honor my ancestors by living fully and freely across borders.
- My joy, Rest, and peace are not optional but my birthright.
- Wherever I plant myself, I will find or build community.

You deserve to be whole in your Blackness—without performing, apologizing, or defending.

And the vast and open world has places where you can begin again.

Voices From Abroad

Africa

"Living in Ghana feels like exhaling. I'm not explaining my existence every day."

– Monique, Ghana

South America

"In Colombia, the Afro culture is rich, but I've had to explain I'm not from here more times than I can count." **– Alicia, Cartagena.**

Asia

"In Thailand, people are curious, but rarely rude. Most interactions concern my accent, not my skin." **– Jason, Chiang Mai.**

Europe

"In Lisbon, I'm seen as American first, Black second. It's a strange shift but also a relief." **– Patrice, Portugal.**

Appendix: Resource List

This appendix is your quick-reference library. It's designed to give you the essentials at a glance: links to trusted websites, lightweight templates, and simple checklists. Use these pages when you need fast answers or a starting point. Go to the companion workbook for deeper tools like detailed trackers, fillable worksheets, and expanded planning logs. The workbook lets you write things down, track your process, and customize everything for your move.

Immigration & Visa Information

- U.S. Department of State: Travel and Visa Information, https://travel.sta te.gov
- Schengen Visa Info (Europe), https://www.schengenvisainfo.com
- VisaHQ: Https://www.visahq.com/
- UK Visas and Immigration, https://www.gov.uk/browse/visas-immigration
- Canada Immigration (IRCC), https://www.canada.ca/en/services/immi gration-citizenship.html
- Australia Immigration, https://immi.homeaffairs.gov.au
- Mexico Immigration (INM),https://www.gob.mx/inm
- Portugal Immigration (SEF), https://imigrante.sef.pt/en
- Thailand Immigration Bureau, https://www.immigration.go.th

International Health Insurance Providers

- SafetyWing, https://safetywing.com
- IMG Global, https://www.imglobal.com
- Allianz Travel, https://www.allianztravelinsurance.com
- Cigna Global, https://www.cignaglobal.com

Travel Safety & Emergency Apps

- Savvy Traveler (U.S. State Department), https://travel.state.gov/content /travel/ en/international-travel.html
- Sitata Travel Safe, https://www.sitata.com
- WhatsApp Live Location, https://www.whatsapp.com
- Red Cross First Aid App, https://www.redcross.org/get-help/how-to-prepare-for-emergencies/mobile-apps.html

Expat Communities and Forums

- **InterNations**, https://www.internations.org
- **Black Women Expats**, https://www.facebook.com/groups/blackwomen expats
- **Expat.com,** https://www.expat.com
- **Facebook:** Black Americans Living Abroad, https://www.facebook.com/ groups/blackamericanslivingabroad
- **Meetup.com:** Find events and social groups for newcomers
- **Download Xpat App:** Join our community by downloading **The Xpat App** for free on the **Apple App Store** (iPhone) or **Google Play Store** (Android) and become a part of the largest global directory of Black expats and nomads, with representation from over 160 countries & territories across the globe.

Tip: To find additional Facebook Groups Search "[Country] Expats" or "[City] Black Expats" for local support networks

Financial & Banking Abroad

- **Wise** (International Banking), https://wise.com
- **Revolut**, https://www.revolut.com
- **Charles Schwab Bank** (U.S. expat-friendly),https://www.schwab.com
- **Remitly** (International Money Transfers),https://www.remitly.com

Mail & Virtual Address Services

- **Traveling Mailbox**, https://travelingmailbox.com
- **iPostal1,** https://ipostal1.com
- **Anytime Mailbox,** https://anytimemailbox.com

Embassy/Consular Services

- **U.S. Embassies & Consulates Worldwide** – https://www.usembassy.gov
- **UK Embassies Worldwide** – https://www.gov.uk/world/embassies

* * *

Appendix: Sample Templates

Use this template to sketch your first overseas budget. *(The workbook includes a more detailed tracker.)*

Category	Estimated Monthly Cost	Notes
Housing		
Utilities/Internet		
Food & Dining		
Transportation		
Healthcare		
Visa/Legal Fees		
Entertainment		
Savings		
Miscellaneous		

* * *

Basic Packing List (Starter Version)

This list covers essentials. Expand or customize depending on your country and lifestyle.

- Passport + Copies
- Visa & Immigration Documents
- Laptop + Chargers
- Medications & Prescriptions
- Travel Insurance Documents
- Bank/ATM Cards
- 1–2 Weeks of Clothing
- Lightweight Jacket Toiletries (travel-size)
- Emergency Contacts (digital + paper)

The workbook includes a fully customizable packing planner with seasonal and country-specific sections.

Visa Application Checklist (Generic)

This template covers standard requirements across many countries.

- Valid Passport (at least 6 months remaining)
- Completed Application Form
- Passport Photos (correct size/format)
- Proof of Income/Bank Statements
- Proof of Accommodation (lease, hotel booking, or host letter)
- Health Insurance Certificate
- Background Check (police/FBI)
- Academic/Work Records (if applicable)
- Payment Receipt of Application Fee

For detailed step-by-step visa planning with country-specific notes, see the workbook.

* * *

Embassy Contact Log (Sample)

Use this template to note the most essential embassy and consular contacts. Keep both digital and paper copies with you when traveling.

Country	Embassy/Consulate Location	Phone Number	Email	Emergency Hours/Notes

Tip: Always confirm the after-hours emergency line for your embassy. Some services are limited to life-or-death emergencies only.

The workbook includes a full Embassy & Consulate Log with space for multiple countries, personal notes, and updates.

* * *

Appendix: Contact & Reference Information

U.S. Citizen Services

- STEP (Smart Traveler Enrollment Program): Register your trip with the U.S. State Department for alerts and embassy support. https://step.state.gov
- U.S. Embassies & Consulates Worldwide: https://www.usembassy.gov
- U.S. State Department – Travel Advisories: https://travel.state.gov

UK Citizen Services

- Foreign, Commonwealth & Development Office: https://www.gov.uk/

<u>world</u>
- Find a UK Embassy or Consulate: https://<u>www.gov.uk/world/embassies</u>

Canadian Citizen Services

- Government of Canada – Travel and Consular Services: https://travel.gc. ca
- Embassies and Consulates Worldwide: https://travel.gc.ca/assistance/e mbassies-consulates

Emergency Numbers (Global Basics)

- Europe (EU-wide): 112
- UK: 999
- Australia/New Zealand: 000
- Mexico:911
- Japan:110 (police), 119 (ambulance/fire)
- Thailand: 191 (police), 1554 (ambulance)

International Helplines

- **International SOS (Medical & Travel Security):** https://<u>www.internatio nalsos.com</u>
- **Red Cross Emergency App:** https://<u>www.redcross.org/get-help/how-to-prepare-for-</u> emergencies/mobile-apps.html

Final Word

There is no one "right way" to move abroad; it is just your way. These resources support you, but don't underestimate your intuition, curiosity, and capacity to figure things out as you go.

The adventure of your life is not just in the destination, it's in the details, the planning, the first days, and the long-term dreams you're building now.

Preparation is power. These "small" details, your phone, your lease, your documents, form the infrastructure of your freedom. Handle them now, and you'll be able to land softer, integrate faster, and focus on living with intention, not scrambling with frustration.

You've got everything you need. And when you don't, a world of resources is ready to help.

You're not just moving. You're transitioning into a lifestyle designed with purpose and peace. This checklist is the bridge between your vision and your reality.

Affirmation:
"I am allowed to want more."
"I am allowed to have more."
"I am allowed to be more, on my own terms, in my own time."

Conclusion

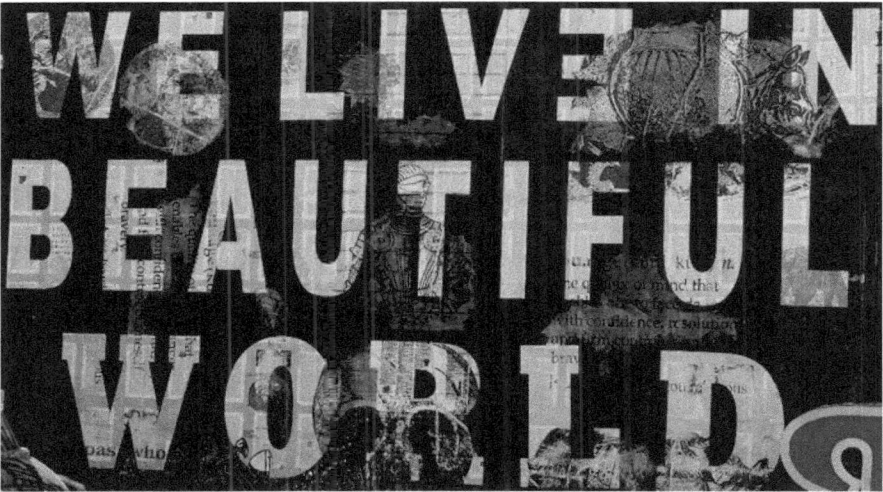

There's a moment, quiet but unmistakable, when the discomfort of staying the same finally outweighs the fear of change. If you've reached the end of this book, that moment may already be here. Or maybe it's on its way. Either way, you are not lost. You are becoming.

You've read the stories, strategies, logistics, and lived truths of building a life abroad, not as an escape but as an expansion, not as a fantasy but as a freedom strategy.

Here's what I want you to know as you step forward:

You don't need permission to want more peace.

You don't need a million dollars to feel rich.

You don't need to stay stuck to prove you're strong.

You need clarity, a plan, a willingness to bet on yourself, and the courage to remember that home is not a single place; it's wherever you are fully seen, supported, and soft.

Leaving isn't failure, and starting over isn't shameful. Choosing yourself, choosing joy, health, adventure, and Rest, is *radical, especially* if you were taught to settle for survival.

Whether you're retiring in the hills of Portugal, building a new business in Ghana, raising your babies in Mexico, or rediscovering yourself in Thailand, know this:

Your attackers have accused you of playing the victim because they are jealous that you are a survivor, a descendant carrying the strength of a long list of ancestors who were also survivors.

You belong where you feel most free.

So book the ticket, research the visa, and sell what no longer serves. Let the whispers become a plan, and let the plan become your new life.

You are not running away.

You walk boldly, tenderly, wisely, toward everything you deserve.

Epilogue

If you've reached this point, you already know—this book was never about convincing you to go. It was about showing you the truth, the tools, and the possibilities so you can make your own choice.

Living abroad isn't a magic fix. It won't erase racism, erase stress, or hand you peace on a platter. What it *will* do is give you options. It gives you the power to choose where and how you live, instead of being boxed into a place that doesn't value you. And for us, as Black women and men, that choice alone is revolutionary.

I won't pretend it's easy. It takes research, paperwork, money, patience, and grit. It takes dealing with culture shock, finding your tribe, and unlearning the idea that struggle is the default. But once you push through, the payoff is real: safety, Rest, dignity, and the freedom to breathe without looking over your shoulder every minute.

If your spirit has been whispering—or yelling—that it's time to go, don't ignore it. Life is too short to keep surviving when you deserve to live.

No one can make this decision for you, not me, your family, or your friends. But if you're ready and if you *can* go, then go.

The world is bigger than the block you grew up on. And your soul deserves to sing wherever it feels at home.

Afterword

Writing this book was personal. It came from my decision to walk away from what looked "comfortable" on paper and trust that my life could be more than survival. Every chapter, every checklist, every story is here, so you don't have to figure this out the hard way like I did.

By now, you know the truth. Moving abroad isn't glamorous every day. It's visas, paperwork, learning new systems, building new habits, and facing yourself in ways you didn't expect. But it's also joy. It's safety. It's peace. It's walking down the street without the constant weight of being targeted. It's living somewhere that lets you expand instead of shrink.

If this book has done its job, you should be holding a map now—not a fantasy, but a real plan. Whether you move next month, next year, or in five years from now, the choice is yours. And that choice is powerful.

Our ancestors didn't get the chance to pick their borders. We do, and that's not something to waste.

So please take what you've learned here and put it into action. Use the workbook, planner, and resources in the appendix to build your community and protect your peace.

And remember this: nobody's going to hand you freedom. You have to claim it.

If you can go, then go.

About the Author

Ajilya Duroji is a storyteller, freedom-seeker, and first-generation American Immigrant who traded in her business suit for a wetsuit—and never looked back.

After building a successful career in the United States, Ajilya felt a powerful, undeniable pull to leave it all behind. In 2021, with no master plan and only her intuition as a compass, she put her life into storage and moved abroad. What followed was a journey of healing, rebuilding, and rediscovery that changed everything.

Now a certified scuba diver, serial entrepreneur, and intentional world traveler in the making, Ajilya has made it her mission to help other Black women unlearn survival and lean into softness, sovereignty, and joy.

Through her books, workshops, and honest storytelling, she provides practical guidance and emotional permission to leave behind systems never built for our flourishing.

She writes for women ready to reclaim their time, rewrite their narratives, and remember that peace is not a luxury—it's a right.

When she's not writing or exploring a new coastline, you can find her mentoring aspiring expats/ or as she prefers to be classified, American Immigrants, building digital income streams, or diving into new depths— literally and figuratively.

To learn more, join her expat email list, or download free resources, visit:

You can connect with me on:
- https://beacons.ai/freedomblueprinthq
- https://www.facebook.com/profile.php?id=61576419634174

www.ingramcontent.com/pod-product-compliance
Lightning Source LLC
Chambersburg PA
CBHW031428270326
41930CB00007B/617